This Book is dedicated to my Father, who taught me this wonderful game and to my family (Lissa, Cooper, Cara, Mark and Sally) for supporting my passionate endeavor.

Contents

I.	The Quest	4	
II.	America's Triple Crown	17	
	- Augusta National		
	- Cypress Point		
	- Pine Valley		
III.	Championship Venues	37	
	- Merion		
	- Oakmont		
	- Shinnecock Hills		
	- Oakland Hills		
	- Oak Hill		
	- The Country Club		
	- Medinah		
	- Winged Foot		
	- Baltusrol		
	- Olympic Club		
	- Cherry Hills		
	- Riviera		
IV.	Historic Beauties	61	
	- Seminole		
	- National Golf Links		
	- Chicago Golf Club		
	- Quaker Ridge		
	- Interlachen		
	- Garden City		
	- San Francisco Golf Club		
	- Somerset Hills		
	- Los Angeles CC		
	- Peachtree		
V.	A New Breed of Excellence	77	
	- Muirfield Village		
	- Shadow Creek		
	- Honors Course		
	- Double Eagle		
	- Wade Hampton		
VI.	Hidden Gems	86	
	- Crystal Downs		
	- Prairie Dunes		
	- Camargo Club		
	- Kittansett		
	- Valley Club of Montecito		
	- Eugene CC		
	- Forest Highlands		
	- Black Diamond Ranch		
VII.	Public Pearls	100	
	- Pebble Beach		
	- Spyglass Hill		
	- Pinehurst #2		
	- TPC Sawgrass		
	- Blackwolf Run		
	- Mauna Kea		
VIII.	Toughest Tickets in Town	111	
	- Augusta National		
	- The Country Club		
	- Los Angeles CC		
	- Chicago GC		
	- The Golf Club		
IX.	My Top 10 Favorite Courses	113	
X.	My 5 Favorite Golf Architects	115	
XI.	Best 18 Golf Holes in America	117	
XII.	Tips to Gain Access	126	

The Quest

The Journey Starts

I started my quest at the age of 15. My father, a master sergeant in the Army, saved all year to pay for a one week vacation in California. His sons, my brother Mark and I, were now accomplished high school golfers living in Tacoma, Washington, and ready to play one of America's finest golf courses. The first top 100 course I played was Pebble Beach Golf Links. Luckily, the green fees in 1974 were $35. Expensive at the time, but having saved most of the year, my father was able to treat his boys to one of the finest golfing experiences in the world.

The next day we played a relatively new course, built in 1966 that was receiving rave reviews. Spyglass Hill was the second course on the top 100 list I played. Without realizing it at the time, I had taken the first steps of a journey that would take 25 years to complete.

The Quest is my journey to play the Top 100 courses in America, as listed by *Golf Digest* Magazine. Since 1966 *Golf Digest* has ranked America's top 100 golf courses, updating their list every two years. The list I completed was the 1997-1998 version. For those who are familiar with golf course rankings, they know the lists often change from year to year. Thus, completing a list is a moving target. Fortunately 70-80% of the top 100 courses stay the same, even though their relative ranking may change from list to list. Courses like Augusta National and Pebble Beach make every list, along with many other venerable courses. By focusing on the top courses, I was able to build towards completing a list. The 1997-1998 version offered me the best chance to complete my pursuit.

Playing all top 100 courses in America is a rare feat, especially for a golfer who is not rich, nor famous, nor in the golf business. I contacted *Golf Digest* after achieving my feat and they commented that only a "handful of golfers" have ever completed a list. This feat is extra special, because I am a "common man," who had no advantages when pursuing this goal.

The short and treacherous par 3, 7th hole at Pebble Beach, on a dream day with no wind and lots of sunshine.

When describing my passionate pursuit, people often wondered why someone would take the time to achieve such a goal. Why bother taking that extra flight and sleeping in a lonely hotel room to play another golf course? Why spend time networking with friends and colleagues to gain access to another private club? The answer is I am passionate about playing the best golf courses in the world, while engaging in wonderfully unique experiences. The courses that are consistently ranked in the top 100 achieve this lofty status, because they are engaging and memorable. Similar to other "crazy" people who want to climb the highest mountains or ski the best slopes or sail the seven seas, I was drawn to experiencing the splendors of playing America's top golf courses. Each course offers a special exhilarating appeal that swells my excitement, like a kid visiting a new toy store.

Whether hitting a crisp 1-iron across a Pacific inlet to the 16th green at Cypress Point, or walking across the Ben Hogan Bridge with my father during the spring at Augusta National, or showering in the same stall that Bobby Jones used after winning the Grand Slam at Merion, I relish the thrill of enjoying unique experiences.

Golf is one of the few sports in the world where an amateur participant can play the actual venue where the top professionals play. It is nearly impossible to play baseball in Yankee Stadium, or football in the Rose Bowl, or basketball in Madison Square Garden, or tennis at Wimbledon, but golf allows participants to play the actual course the professionals play. You can hit from the exact same tee spot that Jack Nicklaus struck his marvelous 1-iron on the 17th hole in the last round of the US Open at Pebble Beach in 1972. You can play the same course Old Tom Morris played in the 1850's to win his British Open at Prestwick. You can even attempt to drive the same 1st green at Cherry Hills that Arnold Palmer did in 1960, on his way to capturing the US Open. Few other sports allow amateur athletes to experience the same venues as the top professionals. It is this ability to follow the footsteps of our heroes that adds a sense of history and nostalgia to the courses we play, making the experience more valuable.

Another reason for my persistent drive was to accomplish a rare achievement. After playing my first 30-40 courses, I was hooked on completing a list and accomplishing a unique feat. Once I made a concerted effort to achieve my quest, I never felt it would be impossible to complete. I was continually optimistic about meeting the right person or networking to the right situation. With the top 100 courses scattered across the United States, there were times I wondered how I would gain access to various top private clubs, but an opportunity always seemed to arise.

Not to say achieving my quest was happen-stance. For certain courses, I worked very hard and spent time brainstorming with friends to determine the best options for gaining access. Once I defined the best option, I would leverage my personal network to obtain the illusive key to that club. Patience was a virtue, but I was also dogmatic at times to make the event reality.

Another important factor in achieving my goal was the manner in which I leveraged my personal and professional network in a tactful and appropriate way. Golf is a game for gentlemen, especially when dealing with the top golf clubs in the world. Even though I was persistent, I would always approach every networking opportunity with great care and graciousness, never overstepping the bounds to become obnoxious or rude.

College Days

After my humble start on the Monterey Peninsula in 1974, I played few other top courses during my high school years. Most of the top 100 courses are located east of the Mississippi River, particularly in the Northeast and Midwest sections of America.

Sharing a precious round with my family at Cypress Point in 1981. Here on the famous 16th hole, with my brother Mark on the left, my mother Sally and father Marvin.

In 1977 I left Tacoma and entered Stanford University. I was fortunate to have garnered a football scholarship, because my family could never have afforded the expensive fees at Stanford. During my four years at Stanford I was able to play many of the top courses in Northern California. Even though I never became a great college football player, being a good golfer made me an alumni favorite. I was able to leverage the alumni network to play Cypress Point and San Francisco Golf Club, while adding the Olympic Club on my own. I was also able to add Sahalee Golf Club near Seattle during school breaks.

In 1981 I graduated from Stanford with an engineering degree and returned to Tacoma to start my career. Although I added a few wonderful courses to my list during college, my total was still less than ten. It wasn't until I decided to attend graduate business school in 1983 at Wharton, in Philadelphia, that my pursuit really accelerated.

Being in Philadelphia put me in the center of America's golf course elite. While attending business school I played a number of great courses including Baltusrol, Winged Foot (West & East), Plainfield, Saucon Valley and Wilmington Country Club. Funny enough I was not able to play the top courses closest to Philly during my business school days, including Pine Valley, Merion, Aronimink and Baltimore CC. Leveraging the alumni golfing network at Wharton was much harder than at Stanford, because there was no sports connection.

During fall and spring breaks at Wharton, my golfing buddies and I took trips to play the top pubic courses in the Southeast, including Pinehurst #2, the Dunes Course, Harbour Town and Wild Dunes in South Carolina, and the TPC Stadium Course at Sawgrass, along with Bayhill in Orlando. By the time I left Wharton in 1985, I had played approximately 20 of the top 100. Still a long way to go.

The challenging 6th hole at Pine Valley, presenting a vaunting tee shot across a vast wasteland.

Professional Vagabond

After graduating from Wharton in 1985 I joined a management consulting firm in Los Angeles. I lived in Los Angeles for five years, playing all the top 100 courses in Southern California, including Los Angeles North, Riviera and the Mountain Course in Palm Springs, along with the great desert courses in Arizona, including Troon, Troon North and Desert Forest.

Great golf is not my only fond memory of Los Angeles, because I met my lovely wife Lissa there. Los Angeles is also where our son Cooper was born.

After five years in Southern California, we decided to relocate closer to Lissa's family on the East Coast and moved to Atlanta in 1990. Being in Atlanta offered opportunities to play courses in the Southeast and the Midwest. We lived in Atlanta for three years, allowing me to play the best Southeastern courses such as Peachtree, Atlanta Athletic Club, Atlanta Country Club, Long Cove, Shoal Creek, Black Diamond Ranch, Haig Point, and the Greenville Chanticlair course in South Carolina.

Being a consultant also offered opportunities for me to leverage client relationships to play such courses as Sycamore Hills in Fort Wayne, Indiana, the NCR course in Dayton, Muirfield Village in Columbus, Laurel Valley near Pittsburgh and, most importantly Pine Valley in New Jersey. Atlanta was also where we added the fourth member to our family, my daughter Cara.

After three years in Atlanta I changed jobs and joined IBM Consulting and we moved to Connecticut for two years. This again offered the opportunity to play many of the courses in the Northeast.

While living in Connecticut I met a kindred spirit in my quest, Dr Gene Greco. Gene was also pursuing the top 100 courses and he became a wonderful ally to access the top courses in the Northeast. He helped me gain entry to Shinnecock Hills, the National Golf Links, Atlantic and Maidstone. I returned the favor by helping him access Quaker Ridge, Wannamoisett, Crystal Downs, East Lake and Medinah.

The beautiful 9th hole at Maidstone, a charming club at the tip of Long Island.

With so many wonderful courses in the area, I was also able to play Stanwich, Oak Hill, Salem, Bethpage, Garden City and Kittansett. Being a consultant, I frequently traveled to the Midwest, which opened opportunities to play clubs like Oakmont, the Chicago Golf Club, Butler National, Inverness in Toledo, Hazeltine, Interlachen in Minnesota, Bellerive, Old Warson in St. Louis, Crooked Stick in Indianapolis, Scioto in Columbus and Canterbury in Cleveland. I also had assignments in the Southwest enabling me to play Oak Tree, Southern Hills, Colonial, Prairie Dunes and Valhalla in Kentucky.

Then, in 1995, we moved again, this time back to Atlanta. By 1995 I had played almost 60 of the top 100 courses. I was now set to accelerate my pursuit to play the remaining courses.

The period between 1995 through 1999 proved to be my most productive era, as I played nearly ten top 100 courses per year. I not only increased the volume, but also increased the quality of the courses I played. This was when I played many of the most recognized courses including Seminole, Shadow Creek, Wade Hampton, Cherry Hills, Castle Pines, Jupiter Hills and Olympia Fields. In particular, I was able to play Augusta National in 1997, which has its own special story.

Frequent moves related to job changes, and being a management consultant were attributes to my pursuit. I have lived in all four corners of the United States, giving me an opportunity to meet members and other golfers who play the top venues.

Being a member of a national practice in management consultant mandated that I travel to client engagements, allowing me to visit many different locations during my work trips. Consulting also exposed me to leading business executives and colleagues, who were members of the most exclusive clubs.

Sharing the panoramic view from the 3rd tee at Spyglass Hill with my son Cooper.

Another key attribute to my quest was the constant support of my wife and family. Although I am a dedicated family man, pursuing my quest did take me away from home. Luckily I often played during the week, leaving weekends with the family.

Achieving My Quest

In the year 2000, I was well in reach of my goal. As the year started I only had five courses left to play on the list and two of them were public courses in Hawaii. The three private courses were tough though, mainly because all required I play with a member. The three remaining courses were the Robert Trent Jones Club in Virginia, Congressional in Washington DC and The Golf Club in Columbus, Ohio.

Powering a tee shot on the 17th hole at Cypress Point. One of the most beautiful holes in golf.

Each venue was a unique challenge to access. The first target I gained access to was the Robert Trent Jones Golf Club. I required the help of a friend whose college roommate was the greens keeper at the club. My friend contacted the greens keeper and told him of my pursuit. The greens keeper was fascinated that I was so close and agreed to find a member to help complete my list. One down, two to go.

For Congressional I enlisted the help of a consulting colleague. Her best friend from high school was now a junior member at the course and she contacted him about my quest. Again, he was happy to help me achieve my unique goal. Two down, one to go.

The Golf Club was particularly challenging, because they have so few members. My friend Dr. Greco came through for me in the clutch. A member of his club in Southampton knew a member at the Golf Club. Once Dr Greco's friend told the Golf Club member about my passionate pursuit he was honored to host me for my final private club round.

As I neared my goal, it was heartwarming to see how other golfers appreciated the grandeur of my accomplishment. The spirit of golf embodied their desire to share in my unique dream, which was very special.

After nabbing the three private courses, the only two remaining courses were in Hawaii, and both were resort courses. I wanted to share my achievement with my family, so I arranged a family holiday to play the Prince Course at Princeville and the Mauna Kea course on the Big Island. We played the Prince Course first and ended with a special round on the Mauna Kea course. My daughter was only 7 at the time, so she kept score, while my 11 year old son and my wife played by my side. It was a wonderful way to share my passionate accomplishment with the ones I love most.

What next for this crazy golfer. My desire to play the top courses has given way to spending more time with my kids and passing on my love for golf the way my father passed it on to me. I was fortunate to have played many of the top courses with my family and close friends, sharing special times with special people. One benefit of playing all the top American courses is that I am close to completing the global 100 list. I have played 90 courses on the list of Top 100 Courses in the World as ranked by *Golf* Magazine. The last 10 will be tough though, because they are in Japan, New Zealand, South Africa, Mexico and a few new ones in the United States. That global Quest may be the subject of a new book though.

In the following pages I provide course-by-course details to many of my favorite venues. I help readers understand how I gained access to each venue, using a variety of methods to achieve my goal. I also provide unique insights into each club, ones that I garnered from members or by just absorbing the ambiance each venue offered.

At the beginning of each section you will find the actual scorecard I used for my round at each course. I have also sprinkled pictures of my rounds throughout the book to help the reader visualize these amazing golf destinations. I hope these revelations will inspire other golfers to pursue their dreams to play America's best courses. The sign may say "Members Only," but I have proven that even non-members can enjoy the mystique and beauty of these golfing treasures.

What Makes a Golf Course "Great?"

Every golfer around the world has their own definition of what makes a golf course great. If you prescribe to the criteria commonly used by golf course ranking entities, there are nine major categories used to evaluate top courses. While I agree with the major categories used, my personal weighting of each criteria is often different than other golfers.

Here is the list of nine criteria used by Golf Digest to evaluate the courses they select for consideration into their Top 100 ranking every two years:

1. Shot Values---How well does the course pose risks and rewards and equally test length, accuracy and finesse?

2. Resistance to Scoring---How difficult, while still being fair, is the course for a scratch player from the back tees?

3. Design Variety---How varied are the holes in differing lengths, configurations, hazard placements, green shapes and green contours?

4. Memorability---How well do the design features (tees, fairways, greens, hazards, vegetation and terrain) provide individuality to each hole, yet a collective continuity to the entire 18?

5. Aesthetics---How well do the scenic values of the course (including landscaping, vegetation, water features and backdrops) add to the pleasure of the round?

6. Conditioning---How would you rate the playing quality of the tees, fairways and greens when you last played the course?

7. Ambiance---How well does he overall feel and atmosphere of the course reflect or uphold the traditional values of the game?

8. Walkability---How walkable is the course in terms of terrain and distance between holes?

9. Tradition---How has this venue added to golf or architectural history?

Golf Digest utilizes volunteer course raters, who obtain detailed score sheets to evaluate targeted courses. They play as many of the targeted courses as possible every two years, using a 1-10 scale for each criteria. Once courses have been evaluated by numerous raters, the evaluations are compiled to provide an overall score for the course, which is then compared to the composite scores from other courses. The courses with the highest composite scores are then ranked in the top 100. A pretty simple metric to quantify the overall "greatness" of a golf course.

For us non-evaluators, each golfer will prioritize the criteria differently, giving weight to those aspects, which they feel are most important. When I play top courses, my top criteria are Design Variety, Memorability, Aesthetics, Ambiance and Tradition. These are elements of a course that I remember and enjoy most. I am less interested in playing incredibly tough courses, unless they also beautiful, unique and memorable.

Although I do not mind difficult golf courses, a great tough course should offer more than a penal design to rate highly. One of the toughest golf courses in America is the Eisenhower Course in Industry Hills, California, with a course rating near 76.0 and a slope near 150, but it is far from being great, because it is not memorable or unique. Also, a course can be extremely beautiful, like the municipal course at Pacific Grove in California, with a spectacular back-nine that plays through rugged sand dunes, but it is not challenging enough to achieve greatness.

A course is considered great when it scores highly on each of the criteria. Thus, many of the best courses are beautiful, tough, memorable and well conditioned. There are over 20,000 golf courses in the United States, so to become one of the select 0.5% of all courses, requires something special.

I found the greatest courses are those that appear as if they have existed for years and naturally integrate into the landscape. This is why so many of the top courses are older designs, built before 1940, because architects were forced to use the natural features of the land and not rely on bulldozers to shape topography. Today, the land given to architects is not always the best for golf, requiring them to move tons of dirt to get the right routing and hole configuration. Only the best architects are able to take a rough piece of property and make a golf course look natural.

Many of my favorite courses offer design features that provide risk-reward shot-making, while keeping the round fun. I enjoy short par fours that provide options to drive the green, but will punish a wayward shot. I love short par fives that provide the dangerous option to hit the green in two shots and putt for that elusive eagle. A number of the older courses offer these features, mainly because technology has shorted their original design, but they make the course exciting to play.

All the courses I discuss in this book are special and fit my criteria for greatness. All are balanced, but normally have a unique aspect that catapults them to stardom. Some are associated with historic events, like a US Open or PGA championship and others are just wonderful private venues that offer a stupendous experience. I do not cover all the 100 courses that composed my Golf Digest list, but have selected 44 that I consider to be most interesting to the reader. I hope you enjoy sharing my journey.

A spectacular Fall day at the National Golf Links, here playing the short par 3 6th hole.

The Top 100 List I Completed
Golf Digest's 100 Greatest Golf Courses in America
1997-1998 Version: In Rank Order

1. Pine Valley
2. Augusta National
3. Cypress Point
4. Pebble Beach
5. Shinnecock Hills
6. Winged Foot (West)
7. Oakmont
8. Merion
9. Pinehurst #2
10. Oakland Hills
11. Olympic Club
12. Seminole
13. The Country Club
14. National Golf Links
15. Shadow Creek
16. Medinah #3
17. Prairie Dunes
18. Crystal Downs
19. San Francisco
20. Wade Hampton
21. Muirfield Village
22. Oak Hill
23. Quaker Ridge
24. Southern Hills
25. Garden City
26. The Golf Club
27. Spyglass Hill
28. Baltusrol (Lower)
29. Peachtree
30. Riviera
31. Cherry Hills
32. Scioto
33. Inverness
34. Maidstone
35. Chicago
36. Winged Foot (East)
37. The Honors Course
38. Los Angeles
39. Plainfield
40. Baltimore (East)
41. The Ocean Course at Kiawah
42. Cascades
43. Somerset Hills
44. Castle Pines
45. Kittansett
46. Interlachen
47. Colonial
48. Forest Highlands
49. Laurel Valley
50. Blackwolf Run (River)
51. Long Cove Club
52. Wannamoisett
53. TPC at Sawgrass
54. Cog Hill
55. Shoal Creek
56. Point O' Woods
57. Desert Forest
58. Butler National
59. Black Diamond Ranch
60. Habour Town Links
61. Valhalla
62. Olympia Fields
63. Canterbury
64. Hazeltine National
65. Atlantic
66. Prince Course
67. Bellerive
68. Oak Tree
69. Congressional (Blue)
70. Camargo
71. Double Eagle
72. Haig Point
73. Milwaukee
74. Jupiter Hills (Hills)
75. Stanwich Club
76. Crooked Stick
77. Saucon Valley (Grace)
78. Eugene
79. Salem
80. NCR
81. Pumpkin Ridge (Ghost Creek)
82. Wilmington (South)
83. Pasatiempo
84. Greenville (Chanticleer)
85. Valley Club of Montecito
86. CC of North Carolina (Dogwood)
87. Sycamore Hills
88. Aronimink
89. Old Waverly
90. Pinetree
91. Troon North
92. Robert Trent Jones GC
93. Troon
94. East Lake
95. Sahalee
96. Old Warson
97. Bay Hill
98. Mauna Kea
99. The Links at Spanish Bay
100. Bethpage (Black)

The American Triple Crown

There is nothing finer in golf than to drive down Magnolia Lane in Augusta, Georgia, knowing you will play the most famous golf course in the world. For golfers it is a near religious experience, synonymous with visiting the Vatican in Italy. Augusta National, the yearly host of the famous Masters Golf Tournament, offers a wonderful ambiance that combines southern charm and a wonderful golf course with a deep sense of golf history.

Two thousand miles west of Georgia lay the most beautiful golf course in the world. Cypress Point is a fiercely private club that has been called the "Sistine Chapel" of golf. It is a masterful work of art that offers a majestic harmony between nature and man-made perfection. The natural panoramic beauty of this course, which borders the Pacific Ocean, offers a mesmerizing fantasy for the golfer

Back across the country to the Northeast, in the sand hills of New Jersey, lays one of the most punishing golf courses in the world. A beacon for the "penal design" architectural philosophy, Pine Valley is a rugged golf course that should only be played by the stern of heart. Another exclusive club that is always rated as the number one golf course in the world.

These three geographically dispersed clubs represent the Triple Crown of American private golf. After playing the top 100 golf courses in America, I can truly say these three courses stand "head and shoulders" above all other venues in the United States.

Almost all knowledgeable golfers, will list these three courses at the top of their list of must plays. They embody the elements most cherished by golfers, including beauty, challenge, history and exclusivity.

They share a number of common attributes. First they offer a wonderfully captivating golf course. Second they provide a rich sense of history. Third they offer a unique ambience that is unmatched anywhere in the world and fourth they are extremely private, making them particularly alluring.

They also have key differences. The courses lie in three different regions of the United States, offering distinct landscapes and, more importantly, different member personalities. They have garnered their greatness via three different paths: Augusta National, with its tournament fame; Cypress Point, with its unmatched beauty; and Pine Valley with its challenging design. Lastly they offer three different architectural styles, each with their own special appeal.

Playing the American Triple Crown was a special feat. It was especially gratifying, because I was able to play each course with my father. He spent his life committed to providing his kids a wonderful life, so being able to arrange these three wonderful trips for him was very rewarding. A nice way to say thank you for being such a super dad.

NAME OF GOLF HOLES
1 .... Tea Olive
2 .... Pink Dogwood
3 .... Flowering Peach
4 .... Flowering Crabapple
5 .... Magnolia
6 .... Juniper
7 .... Pampas
8 .... Yellow Jasmine
9 .... Carolina Cherry
10 .... Camellia
11 .... White Dogwood
12 .... Golden Bell
13 .... Azalea
14 .... Chinese Fir
15 .... Fire Thorn
16 .... Red Bud
17 .... Nandina
18 .... Holly

Augusta National Golf Club

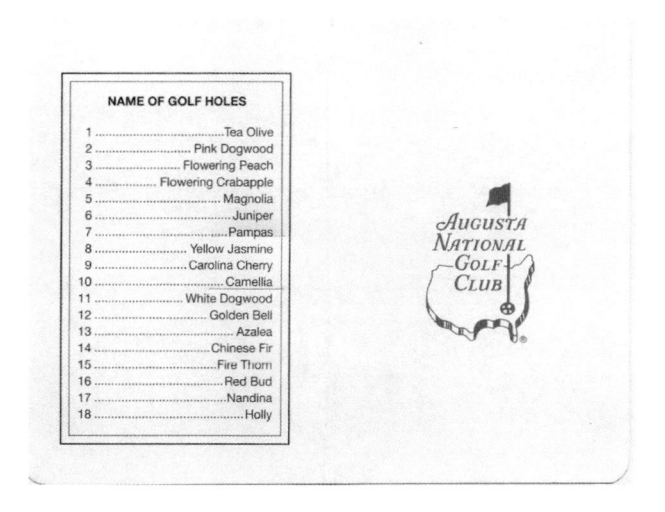

Augusta National

Obtaining an invitation to play Augusta National was like winning the lottery. Throughout my quest Augusta always remained the ultimate prize. In the end it was probably my most challenging and gratifying achievement.

In 1996 I lived in Atlanta, Georgia. Being a member of the business community in Atlanta I would randomly meet golfers who had played Augusta National. They spoke of the wonderful experience as if they had met Elvis or the Pope. It was a shining star in their list of golf achievements.

With a small national membership it was very difficult to meet a member of Augusta National. This club is composed of business titans, like Lou Gerstner, Bill Gates and other prominent corporate leaders. Most of the non-members, who were fortunate enough to play the course, had only played one time and did not have a strong connection to a member. Believe me, I asked.

My lucky break came in late 1996. I was visiting a neighbor, who happened to be one of the starting pitchers for the Atlanta Braves. He was also a golf nut, who had leveraged his baseball fame to play many of the top courses in America. We were discussing the various courses he had recently played and he mentioned playing Augusta National. He knew of my quest and asked if I had ever played there. I said no, and he suggested I contact his member host to see if a game could be arranged.

Also in 1996 my father decided to retire from his second career (after spending his first 23 working years in the Army). Thus, I thought the perfect retirement gift for my hardworking father would be a round of golf at Augusta National.

My father and I standing on the Byron Nelson Bridge leading to the 12th green, the centerpiece of Amen Corner.

I contacted the Augusta member, referencing my baseball friend and telling him I would love to do something special to celebrate my father's retirement. I mentioned his "blue-collar" roots and described how playing the famed course would be the highlight of his golfing career. After hearing my story, the member gladly agreed and we scheduled a rendezvous for the last week of February, 1997.

Immediately after speaking with the member, I called my father with the news. He was tremendously moved by the special gift, realizing how hard it was to obtain an invitation to one of the most exclusive clubs in the world.

We made the travel arrangements and I flew him down from Seattle the day before our intended round. We spent the evening at a hotel in Augusta, eagerly anticipating our experience, like a kid waiting for Christmas morning to arrive.

I contacted the member the day before our scheduled tee time, to finalize the logistics. I asked if my father and I could arrive early at the club to buy some souvenirs before the round. At most private clubs, entering the grounds before the member was not a problem. Not at Augusta National. He indicated I could not enter the grounds until he had arrived. Wow!! In fact
we were only allowed to be on the grounds while he was present. A very unique arrangement, where the member has 100% accountability for their guests.

The next day was beautifully sunny and we entered the grounds a few minutes after the member indicated. As we turned into Magnolia Lane, a guard greeted us and indicated our host had arrived and to meet him on the driving range. Magnolia Lane is a wonderful driveway about 500 yards long, bordered by large magnolia trees, which form a tidy canopy over the road. At the end of the road lies a gracious southern mansion, which is now the clubhouse.

We parked near the clubhouse and were immediately met by two caddies. They asked us to enter the clubhouse and change our clothes and shoes in the locker room. We followed orders and entered the stately mansion. The clubhouse offered an understated elegance. Walls were covered with pictures and mementos of the Masters Tournament and we could have loitered all day, but we were expected at the driving range.

The tough second shot to the difficult 11th green, from a downhill lie.
The 12th green is in the distance on the right.

The locker room was a modest room with individual lockers fronted by a comfortable bench. Like the Masters Tournament, the dominate color throughout the clubhouse is green. We were assigned a locker and quickly changed into our golf clothes. While changing clothes, I noticed a number of the famous Augusta Green Jackets hanging near various lockers. I later asked my host about the jackets, which are given to members and winners of the Masters tournament. He mentioned the jackets are never taken off the premises and are only worn when the member is on club grounds. This rule applied to Masters winners as well.

After perusing the locker room, we then ventured to the driving range to meet our host. He greeted us and mentioned how honored he was to be a part of such a nice retirement gift.

The driving range at Augusta sits parallel to Magnolia Lane. The turf is very tight and finely manicured, much like the course. The end of the driving range was only 270 yards away, with a high fence bordering Washington Boulevard. Our host indicated that during the Masters a number of the long hitters, like John Daly often clear the fence. Thus, we were welcome to try. Despite my best hits, I was only able to hit mid-way up the fence. It was fun to mimic the professionals though.

Standing in the fairway on the 15th hole, a short, downhill par 5 that has been the scene of many dramatic moments during the Masters Tournament. Notice the scoreboard erected weeks before the actual tournament in April.

After the driving range we went to the giant putting green near the first tee. The greens in February were not as fast as the tournament greens in April, but they were plenty challenging. It was amazing to putt on the same practice green that Bobby Jones, Jack Nicklaus and Sam Snead had utilized before starting their rounds. It is hard to describe, but you really feel as if the "ghosts of golfing past" are still roaming the grounds, helping enrich the experience at this special place.

After a few practice putts, we were now ready to begin our round. I played from the tournament tees, along with a friend of our host, and my father and our host played from the member's tees. Another wonderful tradition at Augusta National is that caddies are mandatory for each player. My caddie had been working at Augusta National for 15 years, while my father's caddie had been at Augusta for a whopping 31 years. Both were very knowledgeable about the course and had numerous stories about the membership and the tournament.

Standing on the first tee at Augusta National is almost surreal. Nearly all the golfing gods since 1933 have used this same tee box to start their round. With much anticipation and nervousness we all hit good tee shots to begin our memorable adventure.

The course was in excellent condition. The tee boxes were cut very low, resembling putting greens at most municipal courses. The fairways were also very tight, making it difficult to hit from, because there was little cushion raising the ball from the fairway surface. The rough was non-existent, being added a few years later to toughen the course.

As we started, we noticed the scoreboards for the tournament were being erected, which helped enrich the experience. Our host mentioned the members conduct a tournament before the Masters each year, utilizing the scoreboards, concessions and other services, to prepare the workers for the real-deal in April. The spring of 1997 was also a special time in the history of golf, because six weeks after we played, a young phenom by the name of Tiger Woods won the first of his four green jackets.

Throughout the round our host was gracious enough to take time and tell us stories about the course and the club. On number 2, a long, downhill Par 5, he said not to hit our tee shots to the left. He said they called the left trees "the Delta Office," because if you hit it left during the tournament you are bound to make a high score and need airplane reservations to go home early.

The beautiful, yet treacherous par 3 12th hole playing diagonally across Rae's Creek to a small green. Luckily it was not windy when we played

The front nine at Augusta National, which by the way was the original back nine, is not overly impressive from an architectural standpoint. The fairways are wide, there are few sand traps and no holes utilize water hazards. The real memorable aspect of the front nine is the roller coaster greens, many with multiple levels. Although they were not tournament speed, they were still very fast and challenging.

The best hole on the front nine is number 3. It is a short uphill par 4 that plays to a putting surface that angles away and to the left from the fairway. Even with only a wedge or sand wedge in their hands, the pros struggle to make birdies on this deceptive hole. I hit my tee shot into one of the few fairway sand traps on the front nine. I then hit my second shot short of the green, facing a difficult third shot to the slanted green. My third shot required a delicate chip, which I nearly hit perfectly, but still only managed to leave the ball six feet from the pin. I then missed the breaking putt for a bogey. These delicate little chips and tough putts are what make Augusta challenging.

Another interesting tidbit is that Augusta National has very few sand traps. In fact it only has 34 bunkers, a ridiculously low amount for a championship course. I believe this fact highlights the brilliance of Alistair Mackenzie, who did not base his design on placing hundreds of sand traps around the course, but rather leveraged the natural features of the land to create his championship venue. I feel today's architects place far too many bunkers on their new courses, instead of creating attractive chipping areas and other more compelling hazards to challenge the golfer.

The back nine at Augusta National is where the real fun starts. The back nine is probably the most famous nine holes in the world, given its exposure on television during the four days of the tournament.

Another interesting point is that all the holes are named for a flower or tree, similar to the tradition in Scotland, where holes are named after their most unique design feature. The names of each hole can be found on the scorecard at the beginning of this chapter.

Hole number 10 starts near the clubhouse and is bordered by the Augusta cottages on the left, which are named for famous members, such as Bobby Jones and Dwight D. Eisenhower. In fact the cottages are used for members and their guests, so if you get the chance to play Augusta National, ask your member about renting the cottages for a night or two.

The best tee shot on number 10 is to hit a hook down a steep hill to position your second shot into a long green that sits below the fairway. One of the few original "Mackenzie Bunkers" still remains in the fairway of number 10. Alistair Mackenzie designed the golf course in 1933, but it has constantly been transformed through the years.

I hit a nice drive that crawled over the crest of the hill and ran another 40 yards toward the green. Although the hole measured 470 yards, I was only left with 170 yards to the green, because the hill had helped my ball reach a length of 300 yards. I pushed my 7-iron into the right greenside bunker, before blasting out and two putting for my bogey.

Number 11 starts the famous "Amen Corner" of the golf course. The tee shot is slightly uphill, before starting downhill after about 200 yards. The distinguishing factor about the tee shot was that pine trees on both sides of the fairway created a very narrow chute to drive through. You had to hit the ball fairly straight, without much curve. This was a feature you never see on television. After hitting my drive into a the fairway, the approach shot to this 450 yard hole is downhill to a green set hard against a pond on the left. I hit a 5-iron short and right of the green. I then chipped to within 5 feet and made the putt for a tough par. When watching the Masters a few weeks after we played, a number of professionals played the hole exactly the same way.

Number 11 also personifies two distinct qualities of Augusta National you never hear about until you play the course. First the entire course sits on the side of a hill, which runs from hits highest point at the clubhouse to the lowest point to Amen Corner. The Amen Corner holes are cut around Rae's Creek, so the elevation change from the 10th tee to the 11th green is significant, testing your endurance. The second point is that you never get a level lie in the fairways. Every shot you hit is from an uneven lie, with the ball below or above your feet, making good shot making a challenge.

On the 11th our host told us a wonderful story about how the members tee for the hole had been moved by a past chairman. The Chairman decided to move the tee away from the championship tee to a location closer to the top of a hill. The new tee made the hole much easier and a number of members were upset by the move. They asked the chairman why he relocated the tee box to the new location. The chairman laughed and said the question reminded him of a situation he encountered while living in Charlotte. The citizens in Charlotte were getting a new airport and asked the mayor why he located the airport so far from the city. The mayor said "why don't be silly. We located the airport in that location, because that is where the planes are going to land." "Thus," the chairman said, "to answer your question, I moved the tee box to the new location, because you will be teeing off from there!! Any other silly questions!!" A benevolent dictator at his best.

The best holes at Augusta National are the 12th and 13th. The 12th is a short par 3 that plays across Rae's Creek to a small green. The 13th is a short par 5 that curls around Rae's Creek on the drive and then crosses over Rae's creek for the approach shot. Two wonderful holes that challenge your golfing skills, while leading you past a boutique of breathtaking azaleas and flowers.

My father hitting his third shot to the large green, across Rae's Creek at number 13.

During our round, number 12 was playing 150 yards, so I decided to hit a nine-iron. The flagstick was located on the right side of the green, a favorite final round pin placement during the Masters. Thus, the shot had to be precise. Unfortunately I hit the shot a bit thin and plopped into the water. I immediately recalled Tom Weiskopf taking a 13 on the hole during one tournament and did not want to repeat his fate. I then struck my second tee shot well and ended up 20 feet left of the pin, two-putting for my double bogey. My father was a bit more skilled, hitting his seven-iron tee shot into the front bunker and then playing two good shots to save his par.

Number 12 is also where two famous bridges cross Rae's Creek. The Byron Nelson and Ben Hogan bridges honor two past Masters champions and are perfect places for taking memorable pictures. Our host indulged us as we snapped numerous photos crossing the bridge with the 12th green in the background.

The 13th is my favorite hole on the course. It is not long, but extremely strategic. The most desired tee shot is to hit a draw-shot and bend it around the creek to the left. I hit a good drive, but it did not hook to the left, which put me in the trees, through the fairway. I was able to punch a shot to the fairway and play a nice wedge to the green. The pin was tucked in the front right corner of the green, so getting my par was very satisfying. My father was not so lucky, hitting his 3rd shot into Rae's creek and ending up with a double bogey seven.

While playing each hole on the back nine, I could not help but think about all the memorable shots that had been played on these holes. Larry Mize chipping in on the 11th hole to beat Greg Norman, Fred Couples playing a short pitch on number 12 from the steep river bank to salvage par, Curtis Strange failing to hit his ball out of the creek on number 13 on a way to a double bogey and losing his lead on the last day of the tournament. On the 15th and 16th, watching Jack Nicklaus make eagle-birdie on his way to a win in 1986 for his last Masters title. On the 17th watching Ray Floyd bogey the hole and eventually lose in a playoff to Nick Faldo. Watching Arnold Palmer birdie the last hole to win another Masters title. It was wonderful to get a sense of these events by playing the same holes as the professionals and seeing how difficult certain shots must have been.

From the 17th tee to the 18th green, I was again amazed at the steep climb we endured. The Masters is not only a test of golfing skills, but also a test of physical stamina, especially in the final round. The climb over the last two holes is very noticeable, and thank goodness we had caddies to carry our clubs.

On 18, I wanted to finish the round with solid shots. I hit a perfect drive that curved slightly from left to right and found the middle of the fairway. The pin was located on the front left edge near the bunker, similar to where it normally sits during the final round of the Masters. I decided to hit a seven iron to the green, which landed short right onto the fringe of the green. As we walked up the final fairway, we could imagine the thousands of fans cheering for the leader as he approached his final putts to finish the tournament. It was fun to pretend that my putt could be for the Masters title. I stroked it nicely, but unfortunately missed. Another Masters title lost.

Another interesting aspect of Augusta is how differently things appear in real-life as compared to television. On television the 18th green looks big, surrounded by thousands of fans, but in reality it is very average, to almost small. It has two levels, but each level is quite reserved. The grandness of the tournament makes everything seem larger than life on television.

After tapping in for par on the 18th we thanked our host and entered the clubhouse. He provided us a brief tour, showing us the Masters trophy and other Masters' artifacts. We then visited the pro shop and purchased nearly every item known to man that contained a Masters logo. We ended the day having a cool drink in the men's grill with our fabulous host to cap-off a wonderful day.

On the way back to Atlanta, my father and I reflected on our magical day. We realized how fortunate we were to have played Augusta National. What a wonderful retirement gift for us to share.

Pine Valley

Pine Valley has been called the hardest course in the world and after playing many of the best courses, I can confirm its unique stature in the world of golf. It combines a unique penal design, with a beautifully unkempt appeal making Pine Valley so very special.

Pine Valley is a very private club that does not host any professional tournaments. Built in 1918, it has a slightly larger membership than Augusta, with many of the members living in the Northeast. Like Augusta it is a men's only club, where you must play with your host.

While working for Ernst & Young in the early 1990's, I met a Consulting Partner who lived in the Philadelphia area. He was an avid golfer who owned a number of golfing memberships, including one at Pine Valley.

I contacted him about playing Pine Valley and he stated he only uses the club to host clients, so if I wanted to play, I needed to secure a worthy client. Given the fame of Pine Valley I easily secured an executive from Indiana to join me for a round. Since we only had three in our foursome, I made a special request to the Partner to see if my father could join us. Lucky enough, he agreed and I flew my father into Philadelphia to join us for a memorable round

*My father and I playing the diabolical 10th hole at Pine Valley,
my favorite hole on the course.*

We played in late fall of 1993. Like Augusta the property is guarded by a high fence and a guard. In fact Pine Valley is a private community, with its own security force. A number of homes are scattered throughout the property, but none are visible from the course.

My father and I arrived at the course and gave our names to the guard. Unlike Augusta we could enter the property without the member being present. We drove past the 18th and 5th holes and we immediately could see why the course is so special. Each fairway and green is surrounded by waste area and sand dunes. The velvet fairways and greens were framed nicely by brown sand and different shades of scrubby trees and bushes.

As we entered the parking lot, we were greeted by the starter. The parking lot next to the clubhouse is very small, so we grabbed our golfing items and the car was taken to a remote parking location. He asked the name of our host and invited us to enter the clubhouse and locker room area.

The facilities at Pine Valley are very rustic. The clubhouse looks like an old hunting lodge, with cozy arm chairs and worn lockers. We quickly changed into our golf gear and went straight to the pro shop. Like Augusta we spent far too much on everything that contained a course logo.

My client and the member soon joined us and we first had lunch in the grill. The signature dish at Pine Valley is turtle soup, which we all ordered, along with having a hefty sandwich.

After lunch we went to the driving range, which is a mile from the clubhouse. They shuttled us from the clubhouse to the range and back. After hitting a few warm-up balls and practicing our putting, we returned to the clubhouse and the first tee.

The first hole is a dogleg right completely bordered by wasteland. We all hit good drives to start our adventure. Every hole at Pine Valley is stunning. Number 2 is a short, uphill par 4 with a green carved into the top of a sand hill. Number 5 is a daunting par 3 that measures 230 yards playing across a pond. Number 7 is a majestic par 5 that plays from grass island to grass island, across a waste area called "hell's half acre."

Dad teeing off on number 15, a difficult par 5 measuring over 575 yards.

Number 7 is one of only two par 5 holes at Pine Valley and both are over 570 yards long. Having only two par 5 holes, both of which are very long and difficult, is another reason why it is hard to finish with a good score at Pine Valley.

By the way, another unique aspect of Pine Valley is there are no sand trap rakes on the course when you play. The waste areas are never raked, but the traps are raked in the morning and then not raked during the day. After playing from a trap, the player is asked to smooth over the sand impressions, using his club or foot. This creates some difficult lies in the bunkers, especially if the players before you were sloppy about their bunker maintenance.

On the front nine my favorite hole is number 3, a medium length par 3 measuring 165 yards. The tee shot is downhill to a green that is completely surrounded by sand and bushes. I hit an eight-iron and found the green, but was a long way from the pin. Once I reached the green I noticed the pronounced slope and contour I needed to navigate, having to traverse two wicked ridges to reach the hole. Unfortunately it took me an embarrassing four putts to conclude the hole, leaving me with a double bogey five.

The back nine is nothing short of spectacular. Starting with my favorite hole on the course, number 10. The 10th is a 140 yard par 3 with a green that sits like a green billiards table encased in white sand. The front portion of the green is guarded by a deep pot bunker that is affectionately called "the devil's edifice." I hit a nice 9-iron onto the green and made birdie, which added to my admiration of the hole. My father hit an 8 iron into the deep pot bunker and took 3 hacks to get out. His six was not as fun as my two.

Along with number 10 the back nine possesses some engaging holes. Number 13 is a long par 4 that bends to the left, with a green that sits precariously on the edge of a sand dune. Number 14 is a stunning downhill par 3 that plays over a tranquil pond. The scenery was quite spectacular in October with the colorful leaves embracing the green. Number 17 is a wonderful short par 4 and the 18th hole is a classic finishing hole, which plays across a pond on the last shot.

On a clear day you can see the skyline of Philadelphia from the 18th tee. I hit a nice 3-wood from the tee, leaving me 170 yards to the pin. I then hit a solid seven-iron to about 10 feet. The 18th green is a punch bowl, which funnels all approach shots towards the pin. I stoked my best putt of the day and made birdie. A wonderful finish to a punishing round.

Although Pine Valley is very demanding, it is not overbearing. Even when I was hitting shots from the waste areas, I never felt the course was unfair or that I didn't deserve to be punished for my errant shots. Like a tough, disciplined basketball coach, the course made you work hard, but good efforts were rewarded, while poor execution was punished.

After finishing the round our host mentioned that Pine Valley members have a local bet. The bet states that no guest will shoot under 90 on their first attempt to play the course, regardless of their handicap. Following my birdie on 18, I can proudly state I shot 81 for my first round, but my father was not as fortunate, shooting a 94.

What makes Pine Valley truly unique is every hole is routed through waste areas and jungle, with only the tee, fairway and green being a golfer's salvation along a dangerous route. It is similar to playing a Nintendo video game, where Mario bounces from safe spot to safe spot, avoiding the fire, alligators and man-eating flowers. A truly entertaining and rewarding effort if you survive the journey.

Cypress Point

Cypress Point is quite simply the most beautiful golf course in the world. The 16th hole in particular offers the single greatest tee shot in golf. While Pine Valley offers 18 challenging tests of golf, Cypress Point offers a variety of holes that are fun to play and greatly appealing to the eye.

During my senior year at Stanford in 1981 I had the pleasure of playing the exclusive San Francisco Golf Club, courtesy of a supportive Stanford alumnus, who knew me from the football team. While playing the 18th hole at San Francisco, I noticed a man hitting balls across the fairway to a caddie waiting in the adjacent 10th fairway. As I got closer I recognized the gentlemen as a member of the United States Golf Association's Executive Committee. He was also a Stanford Alumni.

As I walked closer to him, I took the opportunity to introduce myself as a fellow Stanford-man and avid golfer. We spoke for a few minutes and I bid him farewell.

This chance meeting proved to be my key to accessing Cypress Point. After returning to campus I discovered the gentleman I met was also a member of Cypress Point. My graduation date was fast approaching, so I decided to contact him to inquire whether he would be willing to sponsor me and my family for a round at Cypress. I called and reminded him of our meeting at the San Francisco Golf Club, which he quickly recalled. I then asked if he would sponsor my family for a round at Cypress Point to celebrate my college graduation. He gladly offered to help.

The picturesque 13th hole at Cypress Point, playing through rugged dunes.

Cypress Point is one of many top clubs that allow non-members to play, without the member being present. My sponsor called the pro shop and arranged everything for our trip. I was able to pay the fees at the time I played, alleviating any payment concerns for my host. This is a wonderful convenience that some clubs offer their members, making it easier for non-members to experience these masterpieces.

After my graduation ceremony we drove two hours to our hotel in Monterey and prepared for our special round. The next morning we drove from Monterey to the gate of the Del Monte Forest and the famous 17-Mile Drive. Entering the Del Monte Forest is like entering an amusement park for golf. It is a virtual golfing playground, offering a potpourri of fabulous golf. The Del Monte Forest is not only home to Cypress Point, but also contains six other stunning courses, including Pebble Beach, the Monterey Peninsula Club, Spanish Bay and Spyglass Hill. The entire community was built to offer first class golf in a naturally beautiful setting, providing an intoxicating nectar of golf at its best. Often, your only companion when playing are the deer walking through the forest or on the fairways.

There are no gates or fences surrounding Cypress Point. The course is quite accessible once you enter the Del Monte Forest. The stately clubhouse sits on a hill overlooking the course. We entered the parking lot and removed our gear from the car. No guard or starter to greet us here. We entered the small professional shop adjacent to the clubhouse. Cypress Point does not allow non-members into the clubhouse, but offers a small locker room for guests.

The professional shop is only 150 square feet, but is stuffed with apparel and accessories displaying the Cypress logo. We were greeted by the professional and assigned our caddies.

My father had injured his knee earlier that year, so he required a motor cart, which initially caused a problem, given the club prefers golfers to walk, with caddies. Luckily he was given a cart and my mother, who does not golf, was able to ride along with me, my brother and father, to share a real family treat.

The first hole is a nice starter, because it plays downhill, with a wide, receptive fairway awaiting the tee shot. The course starts inland for the first 5 holes, weaving through a variety of topography, including massive dunes and wispy grasslands. Number 6 finally turns back to the sea, with numbers 7 to 9 playing through vast sand dunes. A unique architectural feature on the front nine is that two of the par 5 holes are back-to-back at number 5 and 6, a routing feature you rarely see.

My father hitting a full wedge to the panoramic 15th.

My favorite hole on the front nine is number 9, a short, 300-yard par 4, with a long sinuous green set into a sprawling dune. The green is drivable from the tee, but the shot must be precise, navigating the dunes and a massive sand-trap fronting the left side of the green. My brother drove the ball onto the right side of the green and was able to two-putt for his birdie.

I was not as lucky, hitting my tee shot into the right dunes and struggling for my par. My father hit a 5-wood from the tee and hit his pitch shot close, before 2-putting for his par. Three different ways to play the hole, which shows why number 9 is such a strategic masterpiece.

The back-nine starts with the last par 5 hole at number 10. The front nine has three par 5's, and the back-nine has only one. The 10th and 11th are parallel holes that meander through the large cypress firs that border the fairways. Holes 12 through 14 work directly towards the ocean, cutting through tall grasslands and dunes. They offer a variety of shots and terrain.

Number 15 is the start of a wonderful set of three cliffside holes. It is a short 133 yard par 3 with a green tucked on the edge of a cliff, surrounded by artfully crafted bunkers. We all used pitching wedges to the green and luckily achieved par. Number 15 and 16 offer another unique quirk at Cypress Point. Similar to the front nine abnormality, the back nine has back-to-back par 3 holes.

Number 16 is my favorite hole in the world. A spectacular 233 yard par 3 that plays across the angry sea to a small green perched on the edge of a cliff. We were fortunate that only a slight breeze was present when we played, because in a gale the hole would play like a par 4. When playing the best courses, it is always nice to perform well on the signature hole, garnering special bragging rights for the round. I decided to hit a 1-iron on the 16th, because I had been hitting the club well all year and the yardage was perfect. I luckily hit a solid shot, but it went into the right bunker. At least I made it across the chasm. My brother hit a 4-wood and also made the green, as did my father, who hit 3-wood. The entire family had succeeded in reaching land on the other side of the small inlet. I was not able to make my par, but my father and brother both walked away with bragging rights, making par on this daunting hole.

Number 17 is almost the equal of number 16 in beauty and design. It is a 375 yard par 4 that doglegs to the right, along the coastline. The tee shot must transverse a small inlet, while the second shot must be precisely struck, so the ball will not spill into the Pacific. A small grove of gnarled cypress trees are positioned 100 yards short of the green, forcing the golfer to hit a high shot over these imposing sentinels. A wonderfully challenging hole that is also gorgeous.

My brother Mark launching a 3-wood to the 16th, the best One-shot hole in golf.

I decided to tee off with a 3-wood on number 17 to provide more accuracy. I hit a solid shot that found the middle of the fairway. The second shot is very imposing, given the bushy cypress trees that front the green. I hit a high 9-iron onto the green, 15 feet short of the pin. I was eager to garner a birdie, but my putt went racing by the hole, leaving me with a satisfying par.

The 18th is somewhat anti-climatic after playing the three cliff-side wonders. 18 is a short par 4 that bends from left to right up a small hill towards the clubhouse. The landing area for the tee shot is partially hidden and the second shot must negotiate overhanging trees protecting the green. The green is very sloped from front to back, leaving unfair downhill putts, which I navigated poorly to finish my round with a bogey.

Despite the weak 18th hole, we had just concluded one of the most exhilarating rounds of our lives. Cypress Point is not a demanding course like Pine Valley, nor as famous as Augusta National, but it does offer the most beautiful setting for golf anywhere. In 1928, the architect Alistair Mackenzie created an architectural masterpiece that has endured as a stunning reminder to his brilliance.

Championship Venues

Like America's Triple Crown, the courses in this chapter possess many of the same virtues as the illustrious three in the previous chapter. Similar to Augusta National, these formidable courses all garnered fame from hosting major professional golf tournaments through the years. Most are still in consideration to host the United States (US) Open Championship or the Professional Golfer's Association (PGA) Championship, both Major Championships like the British Open and the Masters. I selected these specific private golf clubs, because they all provide enriching golf experiences that are unique and historic.

MERION GOLF CLUB
East Course

Merion

Merion is steeped in history, being the course where Bobby Jones captured the last leg of his Grand Slam in 1930. It is also where Lee Trevino beat Jack Nicklaus in an 18-hole playoff to capture the United States Open Championship in 1971. Over the past eighty years, Merion has been a popular choice for championship committees when looking for a stern, but fair venue to test the best golfers in the world.

While attending Wharton I was never able to garner an invitation to play Merion, but I did get a small taste one winter. On one cold February day during school a close friend and classmate, Tom McCleary and I decided to visit Merion, which is located about 10 miles west of Philadelphia. When we arrived at the course that afternoon, the club was deserted, given the 40 degree temperature and overcast skies. We decided there was no harm in playing a few holes. We pulled 3 clubs each from our bags and played the last 6 holes of the course, starting at number 13, which is near the clubhouse. We were able to finish 18 before darkness and rain halted our march. This brief taste of Merion only whet my appetite for the full dose.

In 1995, a full 10 years after graduating from Wharton I finally got my chance to play the entire 18 holes. While working for IBM I was contacted by a client that Merion was conducting a charity golf tournament, which was open to corporate sponsors. I immediately contacted the charity and we opted to sponsor a foursome to compete in the tournament.

Merion is a quirky course shoehorned into 120 acres of land. Most courses built today average 180--200 acres of land. The course is also bisected by a major road, with seven holes on one side of the road, near the clubhouse and the other 11 on the far side. I assume that when the course was built in 1911, the road was a dirt path for horses. Merion is also the only course I have played that has wicker baskets at the top of their flagsticks, instead of a flag. This was originally done to keep the golfer from gaining an advantage by knowing which way the wind was blowing. Today it is a unique feature of this timeless club.

The clubhouse at Merion is a stately old mansion that looks out over the first tee and 18th green. A giant canopy covers the splendid porch, which fronts the golf course, allowing members to dine, while watching golfers begin and end their rounds.

Merion possesses one of the best starting holes in championship golf. The short par 4 only measures 360 yards, but embodies many of the qualities needed in a fine starting hole. The first tee is located just outside the pro shop, providing an easy walk to the tee box. At 360 yards it does not require a miracle initial shot, allowing the golfer to stretch his muscles and ease into the round. The first green is a large target, although you can not get too sloppy, because sand traps wait to coral wayward shots. The terrain is flat and trees are not a factor. A solid golf hole that allows golfers to initiate a decent start.

The rest of the course is much more demanding and exacting than the first hole. The routing of holes 2 through 12 takes a golfer back and forth across a hilly piece of property on the far side of the road from the clubhouse. The best hole across the road is number 11, which is a 375 yard, downhill par 4 with a green tucked against a creek. This is where Jones completed his slam, winning his match 7 and 6. A plaque on the hole commemorates his unique accomplishment.

After finishing number 12 we then crossed the road again and played holes 13 through 18. The same holes I had played ten years earlier during my school days at Wharton. Holes 13-15 are engaging and cunning holes, requiring accuracy over brawn, but it is the last three holes at Merion that are really special, as they each play across an old abandoned quarry. The 16th is a long par 4 with the second shot playing across the quarry to a large undulating green. The quarry is full of sand and bushes, making it an imposing obstacle. I hit a good 3-wood to the edge of the quarry from the tee. I then followed with a solid 8-iron onto the green, about 15 feet from the pin. The putt was downhill and fast, but I fortunately stroked a solid putt that went in for a rare birdie.

Visiting the historic 11th at Merion during my graduate school days at Wharton Business School. Notice the wicker baskets.

The 17th is a 230 yard par 3 playing from the rim of the quarry into the quarry's floor. The tee shot must clear a small lake to reach the putting surface. A very intimidating sight. I hit my 2-iron just short of the putting green, but was able to chip next to the pin and save par. Two down, one tough hole to go.

The 18th tee is tucked into the side of the quarry, forcing the golfer to hit over the rim to a blind fairway. The 18th is where Ben Hogan hit his famous 1-iron second shot to secure his win in the 1951 United States Open. I hit a solid drive over the rim and into the right rough. The rough was not deep, so the ball was sitting nicely in the grass. I then hit a 6-iron into the right front trap, taking 3 to finish from there, to end with a bogey five. An even par finish on the last three holes, which was a nice way to end my round.

After our round we were allowed to use the facilities and enjoy a nice buffet. The locker room has high vaulted ceilings and old wooden lockers. The showers are probably the best in golf, having large showerheads that pour gallons of water on top of your head, simulating a waterfall. A great way to end a pleasing round on this historic venue.

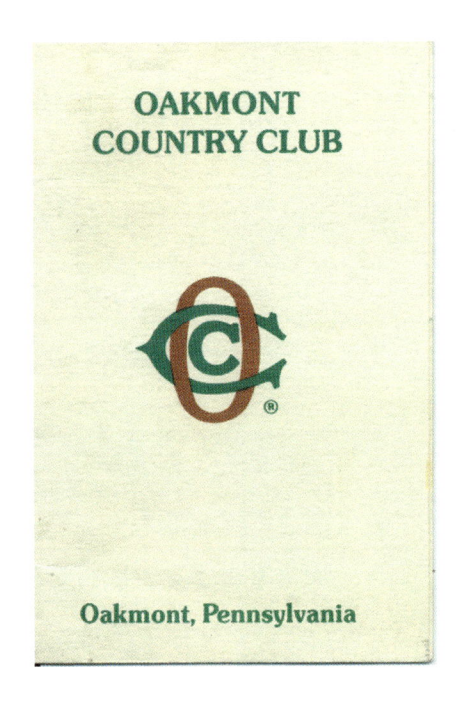

Oakmont

Although Oakmont was built in the same era as Merion, in 1903, the property at Oakmont has allowed the members to stretch the course to keep pace with technology. Thus, Oakmont is still hosting major professional golf championships in the 21st century, conducting the 2007 US Open.

Oakmont is one of the rare championship clubs that allow members from other private courses to contact the starter and schedule a tee time. Only a few days each spring or fall are open to outside play, but at least they offer the opportunity for non-members to play the course. I asked my head professional to call Oakmont to set a date. I was not given a specific time, but told to arrive at the club around 9am. Once the starter knew I had arrived he worked hard to fit me into a group of members, because non-accompanied guests must play with an assigned member.

Fortunately for me, I was put into a group immediately upon my arrival. I had a chance to hit a few practice balls and practice putts before we were on the first tee. Interestingly enough the practice putting green is actually the back of the 9th green. There are 18 little flags situated on the back of the 9th green, with the 9th pin placed up-front. This tells you how enormous the greens are at Oakmont, with the 9th being the largest. They are not quite as large as the double greens at St Andrews, but are just as undulating, while being extremely speedy.

Along with the enormous greens, there are two other noteworthy features. First the lovely Tudor clubhouse is painted a dark green, which is very stunning. Second, like Merion, the course is bisected by a major roadway, with holes 2 through 8 on the far-side, away from the clubhouse, and the other eleven holes closer to the clubhouse.

Oakmont, like Pine Valley, was built using the penal architectural philosophy. There are over 200 sand traps at Oakmont, combined with wicked greens, which make scoring very difficult. In fact, I played four weeks short of the 1994 US Open, which was won by Ernie Els. The course was playing very difficult. The rough was thick and the greens were very firm, to the point that hitting a shot from the rough would almost surely not hold the green.

Unlike Merion, Oakmont has one of the toughest starting holes in golf. The first hole is a straight par 4 hole, measuring 460 yards. The fairway is quite narrow and the green slopes away from the fairway. This hole does not give you any time to warm-up, forecasting more punishment to come.

My favorite hole at Oakmont is number 9, with its' peculiar practice putting area on the back of the green. The 9th is a short par 5 playing uphill towards the clubhouse. I hit my best drive of the day, leaving me only 200 yards to the green. I then hit a 3-iron up the hill into the front greenside bunker. I was able to play a nice soft sand shot next to the pin for a tap-in birdie. My only birdie of the day.

Needless to say the course pummeled me into submission. I shot 89 from the back tees, which was probably the highest score I shot throughout my top 100 journey.

Although I did not score well, I thoroughly enjoyed playing such a tough, yet fair venue. I particularly enjoyed watching the professional's struggle during the US Open, as I had done four weeks earlier.

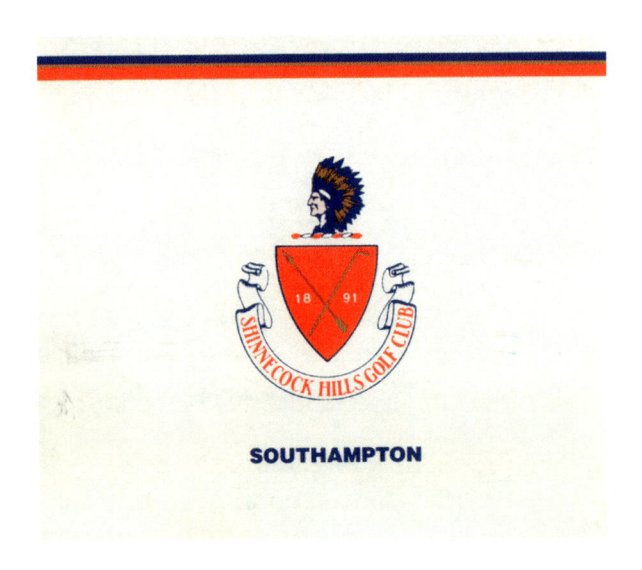

Shinnecock Hills

At the far end of Long Island, two hours drive from Manhattan lays America's greatest links golf course. Built in 1931, Shinnecock hills is a rugged par 70 championship test that has hosted a number of memorable US Open championships, and again host the Open in 2004.

My journey to this windswept dunes area started with a friendly round at a club called Blind Brook in Westchester County, New York. I was invited to play Blind Brook by a friend from Wharton, whose father was a member. Rounding out the foursome was an investment banker, who was a business associate of my friend's father. He also happened to be a member of Shinnecock Hills. During the round at Blind Brook the investment banker offered to sponsor me at Shinnecock.

Like Cypress Point, Shinnecock Hills allows members to sponsor guests, without having to accompany them while they play. I was able to arrange a game in early November.

Approaching Shinnecock Hills Golf Club, you immediately notice the impressive clubhouse perched on the hill. The clubhouse resembles a weathered beach house, made of grey wood and a shingled roof. The clubhouse looks bigger from the outside than it actually is on the inside. I found the locker room small, yet comfortable.

The rugged 18th hole at Shinnecock Hills, a tough par 4 winding through the brown waves of long wispy beach grass.

The day I played the wind was blowing about 20-30 miles per hour. A normal day at Shinnecock. My caddy and I were the only occupants on the course for the first 5-6 holes we played. A wonderfully solitary experience.

The front nine at Shinnecock is solid, but not spectacular. The best hole is number seven, called the "Redan" hole, a copy of the famous Redan hole at North Berwick Golf Course in Scotland. It is a medium length par 3 of 175 yards playing to a green that sits on a ridge, sloping away and to the golfers left. The perfect shot is to hit a nice high hook towards the front right portion of the green and let the terrain take the ball into the middle or back part of the green where the pin is normally located. The day I played I was able to execute my shot in the desired fashion and knocked the ball 5 feet from the pin. Unfortunately I missed my putt, but still walked away with a satisfying par.

Playing my second shot to the green at number 14. It was a cool, breezy day at Shinnecock, but I played well, making a rare birdie on this beautiful brute.

The back nine at Shinnecock has a number of special holes. Number 11 is another exacting par 3 played to a plateau green. Number 14 is one of the best par 4 holes in America. It measures 445 yards playing through a chute of beach berry bushes toward a green set against a large sand dune. A lovely setting, where I birdied, making the hole that much more memorable.

Along with the constant wind the real hazard at Shinnecock is the long beach grass that borders each fairway. Shinnecock reminds me of Muirfield in Scotland. Both are solid golf courses, with no weak holes, yet neither is spectacular or flashy. Eighteen consistently challenging holes to test golfers at all levels. It would be difficult to play this course on a daily basis, especially when the wind is howling, because it requires you to play your top game whenever you step to the first tee.

Oakland Hills Country Club
SOUTH COURSE

Oakland Hills

My Wharton friend Tom McCleary was raised in Detroit and had caddied and played many rounds at Oakland Hills. Thus, after graduating from business school we planned a rendezvous at the famous Michigan course.

Oakland Hills has hosted more major championships than any other club in America. The golf course, was originally built in 1918 by Donald Ross, but was completely redesigned by Robert Trent Jones in 1950 before the US Open. After winning the US Open that year at Oakland Hills, Ben Hogan called the course a "Monster."

Upon entering the grounds at Oakland Hills the first noticeable characteristic is the gigantic white colonial clubhouse. It is one of the largest clubhouses in America. Everything about the club is big. The club has two big courses, a large, spacious locker room and a large membership. It is a true country club, catering to members and their families.

After enjoying lunch in the elegant dining room, we went to the huge driving range to hit some practice shots. The clubhouse areas were beautifully manicured, along with the golfing facilities.

Once we teed off, I started the round on a hot streak. I birdied 2 of the first 3 holes and thought the course was not quite the Monster Hogan implied. Little did I know that this course has real fangs. The greens are very undulating and the fairway sand traps are true hazards, looking like greenside bunkers with steep faces. I quickly gave back the two birdies and finished the front nine in 41. I limped home with a 43 and finished with an 84, one of my higher rounds that year. A testing course that is not overly memorable, but does offer a nice variety of shots.

The best hole on the course is number 16 a medium length par 4 that doglegs right around a large lake. This was where Gary Player hit a soaring 9-iron over willow trees and across the lake to make an improbable birdie on his way to winning the 1976 PGA championship. I also hit a 9-iron second shot, but my results were less spectacular than Mr. Players. I landed in the back bunker and finished with a disappointing bogey.

Oak Hill

Like Oakland Hills, Oak Hill is another big country club that has two wonderful courses originally designed by Donald Ross in 1925. It has also conducted its share of prestigious championships, most recently hosting the 2003 PGA championship won by Shaun Micheel.

Oak Hill allows members of other private clubs to play, provided the head professional of your club calls to make the arrangements. This arrangement is only available during the week.

The first hole at Oak Hill is a real tester right from the start. At 440 yards across a small stream, it requires hitting two solid shots right from the start. I was fortunate to hit two wonderful shots and birdie the first hole. My only highlight for the day.

The rest of the course mimics the first hole. Most of the par 4's are over 400 yards long, with a number of them stretching over 450 yards. A pretty stream meanders through the first half of the course. The course is full of trees, which I understand have been thinned over the past few years to open vistas and playing options.

My favorite hole is number 5, a 400 yard par 4 that doglegs right around a small creek, which cuts in front of the green. A very strategic hole, offering a number of playing options. The rest of the holes are solid, but not overly spectacular, which is typical for Donald Ross designs.

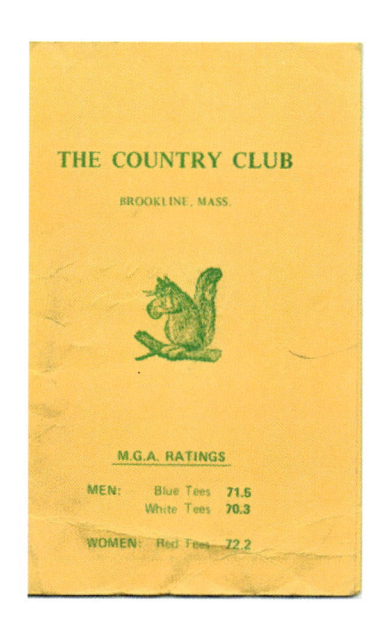

The Country Club

The Country Club in Brookline, Massachusetts will always be a special place for me and my wife. The Country Club is where we celebrated our wedding reception after our marriage ceremony at the Harvard Chapel in 1987. A friend of my father-in-law was a member at The Country Club and agreed to sponsor our reception, as well as host us for golf earlier in the week.

The Country Club is a venerable old club that helped found the USGA in the early 1900's. The course was built in 1902 and has hosted a number of memorable championships, including one of the most exciting Ryder Cups ever, in 2000. In fact the clubhouse balcony used by the USA team to celebrate their victory was where our reception was held.

Given my family had traveled from Seattle to Boston for the wedding, we were all invited to play by our gracious host. The day we played was a wonderfully sunny day in early September. The championship 18 is actually a combination of best holes from the 27 that exist on the property. Fortunately, the number of players on the course that day was light, so we were able to play the championship, or composite 18.

Playing my second shot to the 17th, the hole where Justin Leonard made a monster putt to help the United States win the Ryder Cup in 2000.

The golf course has been lengthened throughout the years, but has kept its design roots from a past era. The tee boxes are square, the greens are flat with the fairway, and the holes follow the natural terrain. The course is also very regional in appearance, with granite outcroppings used at numerous points in the 18 holes, giving it a natural, rustic appearance.

The course is not particularly spectacular, with my favorite hole being number 18. The 18th is a long par 4, measuring 450 yards. It bends slightly to the left, finishing at a raised green, which is fronted by a massive sand trap. The green is positioned in front of the stately old clubhouse, which is a bright yellow. A wonderful New England setting that has seen its share of festive celebrations, including a fun wedding reception in 1987.

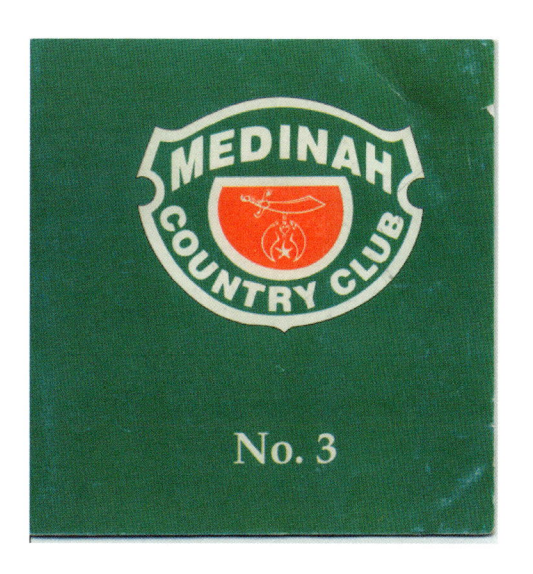

Medinah #3

One of the most impressive and unique clubhouses in the world exists at the Medinah Country Club, north of Chicago. The clubhouse resembles an Arabic Mosque, with a domed roof covering a massive structure. This is home to the Chicago Shriners, who started the club in the 1920's, building a first rate country club that now contains 3 superb golf courses. The most renowned being Course #3, which has held many major championships including the 2006 PGA Championship.

The unique mosque clubhouse at Medinah.

Being part of the Shriner organization, the club has a large membership. The membership is very active and the courses receive heavy play during the warmer months. Medinah is a club that allows members of other private clubs to play without a member, as long as one of their professional staff is playing within the foursome. I had my head professional contact their pro shop and schedule a date. Once I had an appointment, I asked my friends Tom McCleary and Gene Greco to join me to play this historic course.

Medinah #3 has been modified heavily through the years. Little remains of the course originally designed by Tom Bendelow in 1928. The course has been lengthened, re-routed and modified to keep pace with changes in the game of golf. The most distinctive feature of the course is the use of a wide canal on four holes, three of them par 3's. The par 3's play across the canal, creating exciting tee shots over water to small greens.

My good friends Tom McCleary and Gene Greco joining me to play the 17th hole at Medinah, a tough par 3 across a lake.

The other noticeable feature is the course is very long and difficult. Not a fun course to play a leisurely round. My playing partners and I brought single digit handicaps to Medinah that day, but walked away shooting scores between 85 to 92. The course requires length, accuracy and a deft putting touch to score well, which is why championships continue to be played on this difficult layout. My friends and I were in agreement that Medinah #3 is not a fun or memorable course, but it does test your ability to hit solid shots throughout your round.

Winged Foot

Winged Foot, along with Baltusrol are the two most prestigious golf courses in the New York City Area. Winged Foot has hosted five US Open championships and including the one Phil Mickelson lost in 2006. It is a classic example of an American championship golf course and facility.

Unlike British courses, which are famous for their links style, or Australian courses, which are more heath-land in their design, classic American championship courses are parkland designs, leveraging trees and long rough, along with speedy greens to challenge the world's best players. American classics see less wind and quirky bounces, while demanding that the best approach shots are flown into the green, and the preferred recovery is a flop-shot from deep rough. American courses are beautifully manicured and fairways normally offer flat lies.

Winged Foot exudes all these features, having two grand courses and a wonderfully impressive stone clubhouse. The locker room has a large beamed ceiling and rows of old wooden lockers. Every aspect of the club is first class, which is why championship committees always favor Winged Foot for their top events.

While attending Wharton, I met another nice golf soul by the name of John Baity. John was an excellent golfer who had grown-up playing at Winged Foot. Thus, at the end of our first year we drove from Philadelphia to New York to play the course.

Winged Foot is truly a parkland classic. Entering the grounds transports you to a tranquil environment, which seems 1000 miles from the hustle and bustle of Manhattan, which is only 30 miles away.

The two courses at Winged Foot, the East and the more famous West, were both designed by A.W. Tillinghast. To his credit, both courses are ranked in the top 40 courses in America. A rare feat for one club.

Like many championship parkland designs the West Course is very balanced, offering a stern test on every hole. No single hole stands out, except the 10th, which is a long par 3 to a plateau green. This hole embodies the Tillinghast design philosophy, which is to offer a demanding approach shot to a small target, creating difficult recovery shots if the target is missed. I committed a fatal error on the 10th, hitting my 5-iron into the large, steep bunker guarding the front-right portion of the green, short-siding myself with a tucked pin. I could only splash-out to 15 feet and two-putt for a bogey.

Winged Foot offers a wonderful environment for serious golfers. It will test every skill in your game, which is why championship golf organizations are always anxious to hold their tournaments on this high caliber course.

Baltusrol

Baltusrol has hosted more US Open Championships than any other club in America, with its last event being played in 1993, won by Lee Jansen. After hosting seven National Opens, this club in Springfield, New Jersey is a rich part of golf history in the United States.

Baltusrol is a club that allows non-members to contact the general manager to see if he can find a member to host the guest. I had my head professional call the general manager to express my interest in playing, and the GM was nice enough to contact a member to host me.

Like Winged Foot, Baltusrol has two courses, both designed by A.W. Tillinghast in 1922. Tillinghast designed two wonderful courses, the Upper and the more famous Lower. The large, 4-story, Tudor, brick clubhouse sits on a ridge overlooking the Lower course, providing a stately presence as you play your round.

Like Winged Foot West, the Lower course is very demanding. My favorite hole is number 4, a 200 yard par 3 across a large pond. I hit a clean 5-iron onto the green, which left me with a 15 foot birdie putt, but once I got to the green I saw my putt was not so simple. The green is double tiered, with a massive slope in the middle. My ball was on the lower level, while the pin was on the upper level. I stoked the putt perfectly and made a memorable birdie on this marquee hole.

Looking from behind the green, towards the tee of the picturesque 4th hole a 195 yard par 3 over a lake. The imposing clubhouse looms in the background.

An interesting feature at Baltusrol is the use of large fairway bunkers that stretch across the fairway. Tillinghast used this feature at a number of his top courses, including Bethpage and Quaker Ridge. Some bunkers resemble vast wastelands that must be avoided to secure a good score.

Baltusrol is another example of a tough Tillinghast special, like Winged Foot West. It offers a strenuous test for golfers of all capabilities, testing all aspects of your game. It is difficult to delineate between all 18 holes though, which is why I do not rank it among my favorites.

Olympic Club

The Olympic Club in San Francisco is another club that offers reciprocal privileges to members of other private clubs, as long as your club is located farther than 100 miles from San Francisco. While attending Stanford I asked my father to have our head professional arrange a game for me at the Olympic Club.

Olympic is another favorite of championship golf organizations in the United States. It has hosted four US Open championships with the most recent event being held in 1998, which was won by Lee Jansen. The club offers more than golf, having started in 1866 as a full athletic venue that now has over 6,000 members. The club has two courses, with the Lake Course being the most famous.

Olympic has a gigantic clubhouse that overlooks the Lake Course, offering a wonderful venue for weddings and special occasions. The three-story stucco façade can be seen from all parts of the course.

The Lake Course is so named, because it faces Lake Merced, but unfortunately there is no water on the course. The other course is called the Ocean Course, because it faces the ocean. The most distinctive feature of the Lake Course is the thousands of Fir trees that line each fairway. In fact the trees are such an effective hazard that the Lake Course only has one fairway bunker, on number 6. It is amazing that this championship venue only has one fairway trap, and after playing the hole, the trap could be eliminated without degrading any strategic value for the hole.

The short 8th hole, pictured from the clubhouse towards the tee, plays uphill and is completely surrounded by sand traps.

The other noticeable element is the course sits on the side of a hill, falling from the clubhouse to the lake, thus providing hilly lies on every hole.

While the fairways lack any bunkers the greens are a different story. They are well protected by sand with a number of the par 3's being completely surrounded by bunkers. The greens are small and normally very firm.

The course is another solid design, with no weak holes. My favorite hole is number 7, a short par 4 measuring 288 yards. The short length offers a number of playing options, including trying to drive the ball onto the narrow green. I chose this option, but hit the ball into a greenside bunker. I was able to make a nice recovery shot and birdied the hole. One of the few birdie opportunities available on this rugged course.

CHERRY HILLS Country Club

Course Architect William S. Flynn 1922

Major Championships and Champions

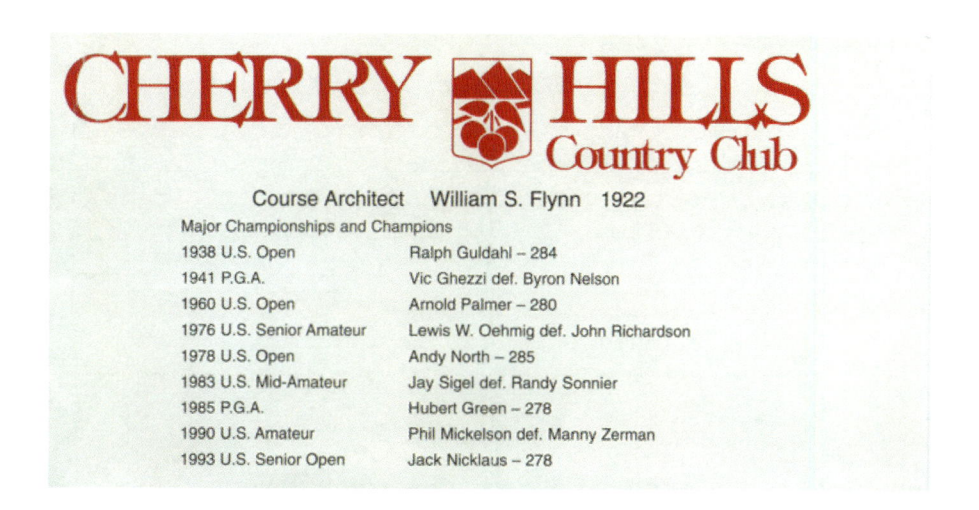

1938 U.S. Open	Ralph Guldahl – 284
1941 P.G.A.	Vic Ghezzi def. Byron Nelson
1960 U.S. Open	Arnold Palmer – 280
1976 U.S. Senior Amateur	Lewis W. Oehmig def. John Richardson
1978 U.S. Open	Andy North – 285
1983 U.S. Mid-Amateur	Jay Sigel def. Randy Sonnier
1985 P.G.A.	Hubert Green – 278
1990 U.S. Amateur	Phil Mickelson def. Manny Zerman
1993 U.S. Senior Open	Jack Nicklaus – 278

Cherry Hills

My path to Cherry Hills started during a round at nearby Castle Pines Golf Club. I was playing in a charity tournament at Castle Pines and met a Cherry Hills member who was in my group. We enjoyed the round and he invited me to his wonderful club the next day.

Cherry Hills is most famous for the final day charge of Arnold Palmer, who won his only US Open championship there in 1960. On the last day of the tournament, Palmer was behind and decided to go for broke on the first hole. The hole measures 340 yards, but plays shorter, because of the thin mountain air, and the downhill nature of the hole. Palmer drove the first green and made birdie, on his way to the title. A plaque describing his feat sits near the first tee box. According to my host almost all good golfers who play their first round at Cherry Hills try to repeat Palmer's feat, so I gave it a rip. I hit a good drive, but pulled it left of the green. I was able to pitch the ball close, but missed my birdie. What a fun way to start a round on a championship course.

The course was built in 1923 and offers a variety of holes. The holes near the clubhouse are very hilly, while holes further away from the clubhouse are fairly flat. The best holes are number 17 and 18, both of which play around water. The 17th is particularly unique, in that the green is an island in a lake. The approach shot must be accurate or a mistake will be very costly.

The clubhouse at Cherry Hills is very understated and warm. The locker room is large, but modestly furnished and the dining areas offer wonderful panoramic views of the course.

The island green at number 17. I tried to hit the green in two shots, but went over into the lake beyond the pin. A tough green on this long par 5.

Riviera

The premier championship course in Southern California is Riviera, affectionately called "Hogan's' Alley." Ben Hogan won a number of Los Angeles Opens in the late 1940's, along with the 1948 US Open at Riviera, so golf writers trumpeted his success by nicknaming the course Hogan's Alley. The club has also hosted the 1983 and 1995 PGA Championships, won by Hal Sutton and Steve Elkington, respectively.

It is the only course in Southern California to have hosted a major professional golf championship. Built in 1926 by George Thomas, who also architected courses at the Los Angeles Country Club and Bel Air Country Club, Riviera has always been a place that attracted and welcomed Hollywood's elite. The wonderfully elegant stucco clubhouse was often used in movies and is a favorite location for corporate and private functions. It still hosts the Los Angeles Open today and is considered by many professionals to be one of the top tour stops.

Riviera is one of the few US Open caliber clubs that offers reciprocal privileges to members of other private clubs. Thus, you can ask your professional to call and arrange a tee time at the club

The approach shot to the demanding 18th green, sitting below the Majestic clubhouse.

I played Riviera during the summer of 1983 weeks before the PGA Championship that year. The course was very difficult, particularly the rough, which is composed of Kikuya grass. Kikuya is an aggressive weed type grass that is rampant in Southern California, having taken over as the primary grass at many of the top clubs. It is very durable, but also very coarse and almost impossible to hit from if the ball settles near the roots in the rough.

My favorite hole at Riviera is number 6 a 175 yard par 3 that is unlike any other par 3 in the country. The unique aspect of number 6 is the green surrounds a sand bunker. Yes, that is right, a sand bunker is situated right in the middle of the green. It looks like a green donut from the tee. The day I played the pin was on the left side of the trap and I pushed my tee shot to the right side of the green. I was forced to hit a chip shot from the putting surface to reach the pin, on the other side of the bunker. I was careful to not take a divot, but it was interesting to chip from the putting green.

Like most George Thomas golf courses, Riviera is solid and balanced, but not overly spectacular. After playing the course twice I still have problems remembering all the holes, even after watching the tournament on television. If you are in Los Angeles and love to play the top courses, Riviera is a must, but do not expect to be "blown-away."

Historic Beauties

The list of top 100 courses is filled with venues built between 1910 and 1932. This era is called the "Golden Age" of golf course architecture, because so many wonderful designs were created during this time. The courses built during that period have withstood the test of time by continuing to challenge the best golfers, while offering a unique old world atmosphere. Similar to visiting an old village in Italy or France, these mature clubs present a window into the past of our great game of golf.

The courses in this section are much more private and reserved than the championship courses mentioned in the last chapter. While they have held championships in the past, they are no longer true championship venues at the highest levels of the game. They will occasionally host special amateur or women's events, such as the Walker Cup or the Solheim Cup, but for the most part they enjoy their anonymity and privacy. I was fortunate enough to gain access to these beauties, which I describe below. They all offer a nostalgic trip to the earliest part of the 20th century.

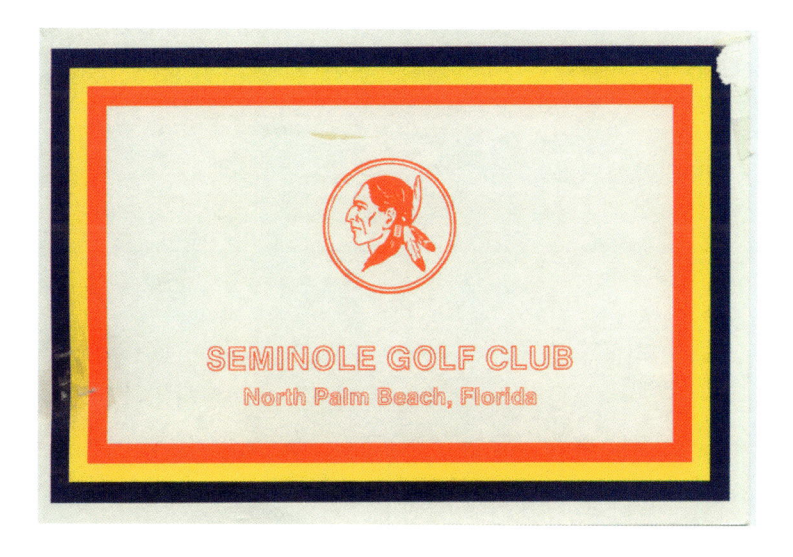

Seminole

Seminole is my favorite Donald Ross designed golf course. Ross designed over 400 courses in the United States, a number of which are listed in every top 100 ranking. This was his best work though, because it goes beyond just offering a strong, consistent design, by providing an exciting playground of memorable golf holes.

The design is also blessed with a nice piece of property, which borders the Atlantic and has a large sand ridge bisecting the course. Ross did a masterful job incorporating the ridge and the ocean into his design. He also offers a number of fun holes that provide a variety of strategic alternatives to the golfer. An example is number 15, a 490 yard par 5. The hole is a dogleg right, that hugs a large lake down the right side. The hole offers two fairways of play for the tee shot, with a row of bunkers and palm trees placed in the middle of the fairway delineating the two paths. You can drive the ball over the water and play a shorter route to the green, or play away from the water and take a longer, safer route. I of course chose the risky route and was able to secure a birdie after a nice drive and 3-iron to the green.

With its location next to the ocean, the course is also very pretty. The last three holes border the ocean, making a wonderful finish to the round. The 17th is a particularly beautiful par 3, measuring 175 yards, playing atop a sand ridge bordering the ocean.

Seminole has a national membership, with many members living in the Northeast. The course is closed during the summer months and is only open from the fall through the spring. While going to school at Wharton I met a friend whose father was a member at Seminole. After graduating, I called my friend to help me arrange an outing that coincided with a business trip to south Florida. His father was happy to oblige, especially since he did not have to accompany me on the round. Like other top courses, Seminole allows members to sponsor guests, without the member being present.

The facilities have a rich, yet laid-back orientation. The pink stucco clubhouse set near the ocean offers a comfortable environment for the snowbirds to relax after a cozy round on their wonderful golf course.

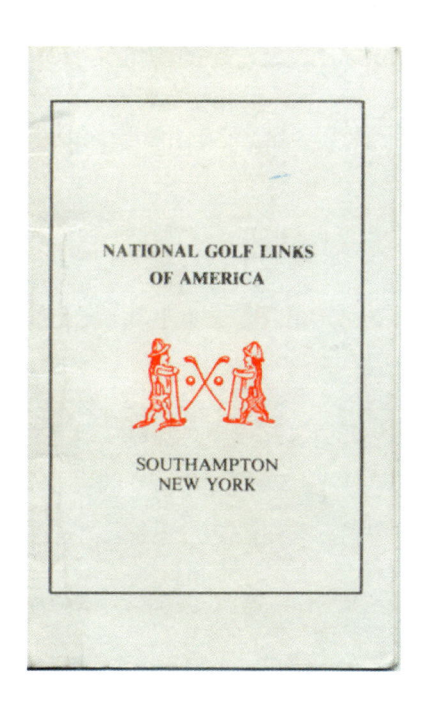

National Golf Links

The National Golf Links is located adjacent to Shinnecock Hills. In fact you can step over a small fence bordering the 6th fairway of Shinnecock and start playing the back nine of National.

My path to National started when I played the Garden City Golf Club, another top 100 course located on Long Island, and met my friend Dr. Gene Greco. Gene also enjoys playing the best courses in America, so we instantly became close friends. During our round at Garden City I mentioned I had a tee time at Shinnecock Hills the following month. Gene lives near Shinnecock and asked whether I would like to play the National Golf Links the same day I played Shinnecock. Although he was not a member, he knew many members, having lived in the Southampton area for 10 years. This was a pleasant surprise, which I eagerly accepted.

I played Shinnecock in the morning and Gene came by the clubhouse after my round to pick me up and take me to the National. While Shinnecock is completely landlocked, the National has 2 holes that border Peconic Sound. The clubhouse at the National is a two-storied grey stone structure that sits on a hill overlooking the course, reminiscent of the grey buildings in St Andrews, Scotland. The other notable structure on the property is a large, Dutch windmill that sits adjacent to the 1st and 2nd holes, which also serves as the club's logo.

National is another course where a member can sponsor your play without being present. Thus, we drove to the clubhouse and stepped to the first tee.

National Golf Links was created in 1911 by C.B. Macdonald as one of the first championship venues in America. Macdonald also worked with another designer by the name of Seth Raynor, who teamed with Macdonald on other championship layouts, including the Chicago

Golf Club. The trademark of nearly all Macdonald's and Raynor's courses is they often copied famous Scottish golf holes into their designs. National has a number of holes fashioned after such famous holes as the Road hole at St Andrews, the Redan hole at North Berwick, and the Alps hole at Prestwick.

Macdonald also created his own famous holes, including the Cape hole, which is number 15 at National. The Cape hole is a risk-reward hole, where the golfer must determine the amount of risk he is willing to take on the tee shot by aiming over water. The hole at the National is a dogleg right that tempts the golfer to bite-off much of the dogleg to obtain a shorter shot to the green. The other famous hole Macdonald developed is called the Punch Bowl. The 16th provides a blind shot to a green that is shaped like a punch bowl, with the surrounding hills forming a concave target that deflects all shots towards the middle.

Playing my second shot to the green on 16, the Cape Hole. Notice the raised plateau greens You can also see the giant windmill in the distance above my club.

Another distinctive feature of their designs is the enormous greens, which are normally set like tables off the ground. Their courses are also very heavily bunkered, but normally offer wide fairways.

I played well on both Shinnecock and National, shooting 77 in the morning at Shinnecock and 74 in the afternoon at National. These two neighborly historic courses offer one of the best combination plays in golf.

Chicago Golf Club

Gaining access to the Chicago Golf Club was one of my more challenging endeavors. The golf course was established in 1894 and designed by CB Macdonald, before he built the National Golf Links. It has a very small membership that is fiercely private.

Fortunately for me, my college friend Tom McCleary, who helped me access Oakland Hills, is now a banker in Chicago. Being an active golfer, he now knows golfers from all the local clubs, including the Chicago Golf Club. Tom was nice enough to arrange a game for me with his member friend.

Passing through the gates at the Chicago Golf Club is like entering a transportation portal that jettisons you to Muirfield, Scotland. The course resembles a Scottish links course dropped into the Midwest country-side. From the clubhouse you can see the entire course. There are few trees or hills, just emerald green fairways cut through brown waves of tall grass. The bunkering is also similar to Scotland presenting steep faces of sod to challenge a recovery shot, while the greens are large and undulating.

I mention Muirfield as the portal destination, because Chicago is a land locked course with the front nine wrapping around most of the back nine, similar to the historic Scottish links. This unique setting is something special in American golf and can still challenge the best golfers after 100 years of existence.

Quaker Ridge

Across the street from Winged Foot is Quaker Ridge Golf Club. The course was designed by A.W. Tillinghast in 1926, to provide a club for Jewish families that lived in the area or commuted from Manhattan.

While working for Ernst & Young in Atlanta, I met a good friend by the name of Jeff Aibel, who spent his childhood playing at Quaker Ridge. His father is a member and he helped me arrange a rendezvous to play the course.

Quaker Ridge is similar in design to its neighbor Winged Foot, but Quaker is wedged into a small piece of land. The front nine wraps counter clockwise around the back nine, and because of the compact configuration of the property, out-of-bounds (OB) stakes frequently come into play on almost every hole during the first nine. I am not a fan of OB stakes being an integral aspect of the design, but Tillinghast did the best he could with a small piece of land.

The back nine is much more pleasant, with a number of holes crossing a lovely stream that meanders through the property. My favorite is number 11 a short par 4 that offers a green fronted by the stream. Although it is only 375 yards, the hole is very strategic. A large tree guards the left side of the fairway and a large bunker guards the right side, making the tee shot an important element for setting-up a good approach shot. The first time I played the hole, I discovered how precise I needed to be with my tee shot. I hit a good 3-wood, but pulled it slightly into the left side of the fairway. The pin was cut on the left portion of the green, so the tree blocked my shot to the pin. I had to hit the approach well right of the pin and convert a lengthy two putt for a par.

A spectacular Autumn day at Quaker Ridge.
Here I am playing my second shot to number three, a tough par 4.

The other noteworthy element at Quaker Ridge is the slope of the greens. Many are severely sloped from back to front or side to side. This requires players to be very precise with their approach shots to avoid slippery downhill or side-hill putts.

Interlachen

I have always found people from the Midwest to be the most gracious and friendly folks in America. This is especially true of the members at Interlachen Country Club in Edina, Minnesota.

I asked my professional to contact Interlachen to arrange a game for me. The professional at Interlachen indicated I must play with a member, so he arranged for me to play with a nice gentleman who had been a member of the club for 30 years.

It was wonderful playing with such a knowledgeable member, who was obviously very proud of his course and its' history. Interlachen is famous for hosting the 1930 US Open where Bobby Jones triumphed on his way to winning the Grand Slam that year. It has also hosted a number of other prestigious amateur, professional and women's events.

When I arrived the member greeted me in the professional shop and we headed to the first tee. The golf course was built in 1911 by Willie Watson and then underwent a major renovation in 1921 by Donald Ross. The Ross renovation is how the course looks today. The course plays to a par of 73, one of the few championship courses with a total par greater than 72. In fact many of the older courses, like Interlachen have decreased par to 70, changing short par 5 holes to long par 4 holes to deal with players hitting the ball farther toda
The golf course is another solid Ross design, with the best hole being number 18, a long par 4 playing uphill to a sloping green. The tee shot requires a drive left of a pond, before hitting to the green.

After our round, my host proudly provided me a tour of the facilities, before we had a light lunch. The club exuded a regal elegance, showing why it is one of the leading clubs in America. The Tudor clubhouse sits on a ridge overlooking the golf course and is filled with memorability from past tournaments, including a grand painting of Bobby Jones in the ball room. Having a fine host made this top 100 course one of my most enjoyable outings.

Garden City

When I drove into the driveway of the Garden City Golf Club in New York, I thought I had received bad directions. The old, ragged building did not resemble the clubhouse of a top 100 golf course. As I entered the locker room it still looked like a facility that required repair.

Garden City is also where I was paired with another non-accompanied guest by the name of Gene Greco. We both had come to experience rustic golf at its best. We enjoyed our round so much we became good friends, who are still exploring great golf courses together today.

Garden City looks like the same course and facility that existed in 1899, when it was created by Devereux Emmet. Another inland links course that is routed through fields of long wavy grass. The club has done a wonderful job keeping the vintage course looking like it did in the early 20th Century.

Like Interlachen, Garden City boasts a par 73, with four par 5's, but only three short holes. My favorite hole is number 2, a short par 3 playing 133 yards across a gorge.

On the back nine one of the best holes is number 18. Funny enough it is a par 3, one of the few championship courses that finishes with a par 3. It plays across a small pond to a large undulating green. I finished with a satisfying par on this grand old American classic.

San Francisco Golf Club

One advantage of being a college football player is that school alumni are eager to help. Although football at Stanford is not the religious experience it is at schools like Texas or Nebraska, our alumni were always gracious enough to help when they could.

I was introduced to a member of the San Francisco Golf Club by one of the coaching assistants after a big win against UCLA. Alumni are often allowed into the locker room after big wins, to meet the players and relish the victory. During my years at Stanford, we were led by such notable coaches as Bill Walsh, George Seifert, Dennis Green and Jim Fassal. My teammates included the likes of John Elway, James Loften and Darren Nelson. Thus, we won our share of games, which helped draw the attendance of influential alumni.

My alumni friend discovered I played golf and asked if I would like to play the SF golf club, where he was a member. I graciously accepted his invitation and scheduled a round for the early spring, after the football season had concluded.

My tee shot on the par 3 15th hole.

San Francisco Golf Club was built in 1918 by the famous AW Tillinghast. It is a lovely course routed along rolling terrain, only minutes from its more famous neighbor, the Olympic Club. This is one of Tillinghast's more creative and subtle designs. Throughout the years, sand traps have been added and almost 200 dot the property today. Some are gigantic, while others are barely large enough to stand in. Giant Monterey cypress trees are also in play, but I believe their presence is not part of the original design, but have been added through the years.

My favorite hole is number 10, a beautiful par 4 measuring 410 yards. It is a visual delight from the tee box, bordered by large cypress fir trees and a number of massive fairway and greenside bunkers. This hole epitomizes the creatively beautiful design at this very private club.

San Francisco Golf Club is one of my favorite Tillinghast designs, along with Somerset Hills and Baltimore Country Club, Five Farms. These three jewels offer fun golf that is both demanding, but enjoyable.

Somerset Hills

While Baltusrol gets maximum exposure for hosting championship tournaments, Somerset Hills Country Club, a Baltusrol neighbor in New Jersey, is barely known in the world of golf. It is a pleasant AW Tillinghast design, which is one of my favorite courses in the Northeast.

While Tillinghast created a number of brutally difficult layouts like Winged Foot and Baltusrol, he also created a number of fantastic "softer" courses like Somerset Hills and the Baltimore Country Club. Somerset Hills was built in 1918 in Bernardsville, New Jersey. It is a short course measuring 6,600 yards from the back tees, with a total par of 71.

Another Wharton friend, by the name of Ted Leh, is an Investment Banker in New York. One of his colleagues is a member of Somerset Hills, and Ted was able to arrange a rendezvous for us to play. Members must play with their guests at Somerset Hills.

After initially hearing that Somerset Hills was designed by Tillinghast, I expected the course to be stern and rigorous. I was totally wrong in my ignorant assessment. This is a lovely course that meanders through a forest, offering a variety of topography and architectural styles. While some of the holes were reminiscent of tough Winged Foot – type holes, most were artfully sculpted to leverage the landscape, offering a beautiful and fun experience.

My favorite holes are numbers 11 and 12, which play around a small pond. The two holes resemble a living Monet painting with weeping willows and a lily covered pond coming into play. Number 11 is a short par 4, while number 12 is a short par 3, where you hit over the pond. A nice set of surprisingly sedate and stunning holes from "Tillie the Terrible."

Standing on the secluded 12th green at Somerset Hills with my good friend Ted Leh.

The Los Angeles Country Club — NORTH COURSE

Los Angeles Country Club

The most exclusive golf club in Southern California is the venerable Los Angeles Country Club (LACC). The LACC has two noteworthy tracks, with the North course receiving the most praise.

After graduating from Wharton with my MBA, I took a management consulting job with a Los Angeles based consulting firm. One of the Senior Partners at the firm was a member at LACC and invited me to play. We became good golfing friends, so I fortunately was able to play the course on numerous occasions. LACC requires that each guest play with a member, making it one of the tougher courses to gain access.

Like its more famous neighbor, Riviera, LACC is a George Thomas creation. The courses share similar landscape and design features, both being excellent courses that require precise shot-making and a deft putting stroke.

Playing the 11th hole at Los Angeles CC with my wife, Lissa and brother Mark. From this tee you can see the skyline of downtown Los Angeles.

My favorite hole at LACC is number 8, a snake-like par 5 that winds around a dry arroyo creek bed. The tee shot plays to the left of the arroyo, with the next shot requiring a shot across and to the right of the arroyo, which extends the entire length of the hole. Precision is desired over length.

LACC is also known in the area for not admitting actors or people involved with the movie industry. The membership seems to be composed of professionals, accountants and lawyers. If you are in business with one of the top professional firms in Los Angeles, check to see if one of their executives has a membership and try to gain access to this oasis bordering Beverly Hills.

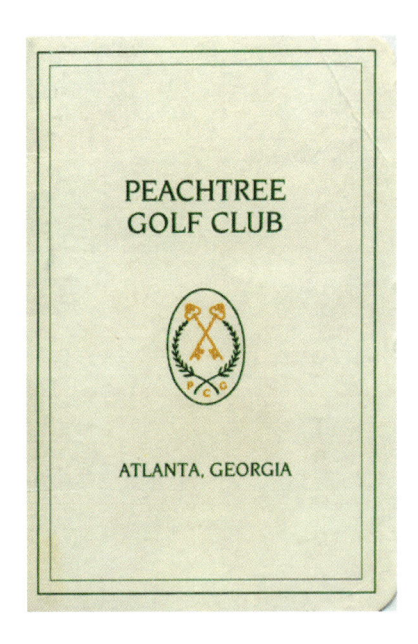

Peachtree

Peachtree Golf Club is the "Grand Old Dame" of golf in Atlanta. It is an exclusive club that has a very small membership and is difficult to access. They do though, offer the chance to play their private pearl, by conducting a number of charity events, which raise a significant amount of money for good causes. Please contact the professional shop at the club to get details. The events are conducted throughout the golfing season.

The golf course was built in 1947, architected by Robert Trent Jones Sr. and the great Bobby Jones. The clubhouse facilities are constructed of brick and are fairly modest, reflecting the club's low-key style.

The golf course is anything but modest. Although many of the holes have a similar feel, there are a number of spectacular holes that help make the course standout. Many of the par 4 holes tee from a high point to a fairway in a valley, before shooting to a green raised above the fairway. This common architectural feature makes it difficult to distinguish many of the holes.

The best hole at Peachtree is the wonderful second hole, a 525 yard par 5. The tee shot reaches the crest of a hill, providing the player a number of intriguing options to play the second shot. A daring player can try for the green by hitting over a lake, while the more conservative player has two fairways to utilize for positioning. The par 3 holes are also all captivating, reflecting the gentile, classy style of this Southern Belle.

A New Breed of Excellence

While the courses in the previous chapter were all constructed before 1932, the courses in this section were all built after 1974. They embody a newer "strategic" design philosophy, which is not as punishing as previous designs, but still very challenging. These courses are also very beautiful, having the advantage of advanced technologies to shape the natural terrain into more visually pleasing environments.

While the previous list of courses became famous for hosting national championships, these courses have gained fame due to their outstanding architectural designs. All five courses were placed into the top 100 ranking from the day they opened, giving credence to their quality. They are also very private sanctuaries, each started by one man or a group of men, who had a vision to create a spectacular golfing experience.

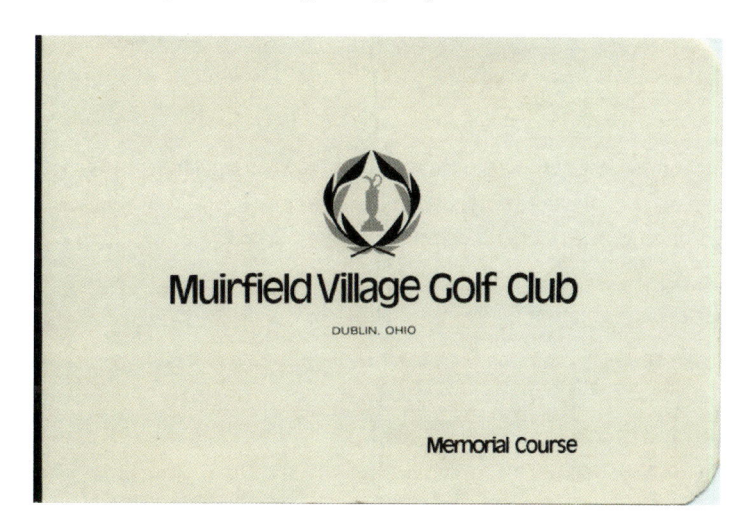

Muirfield Village

Muirfield Village is the course that "Jack Built." Mr. Nicklaus helped create this club in his hometown and designed a beautiful parkland golf course in 1974. It is his finest and most rewarded design to date in the United States.

While working for Ernst & Young I was engaged with a client in Ohio, when I met a Columbus-based Audit Partner who was a member of Muirfield Village. Like the arrangement at Pine Valley, the Partner suggested I find a client to play and he would arrange a tee time. Again, it was no problem finding an eager client to play Muirfield Village.

Unlike most top ranked courses, even the newer courses, Muirfield Village is the centerpiece of a housing development. The golf course is routed through an expensive neighborhood. I was slightly shocked by this revelation as I drove to the odd shaped clubhouse, which looks like a wood pyramid.

After meeting my client and the Partner we went to the driving range to hit some practice balls. The driving range is very unique, because it has four different teeing locations, so you can always hit into the wind. It probably measures 350 yards across and offers golfers a multitude of target choices. If you read some of Jack's books, he states the best way to test your ball striking is to hit into the wind, because only well-struck balls will stay on their intended flight path. Thus, the range was built with this in mind.

Muirfield Village has the reputation among the touring professionals to be one of the most manicured and well conditioned courses on the PGA Tour. After playing the course I can see why. You can putt on the tee boxes and the greens are firm and fast.

The front nine is fun and a good test, but the back nine is where the spectacular holes lay. The 11th a long par 5 is one of the best 3 shot holes in the country. A creek snakes the entire length of the hole, starting on the left side of the fairway, then cutting to the right side, before finishing in front of the raised green. The tee shot must be played left toward the stream to offer a shot at hitting the green in two. The hole offers many strategic options and is exciting to play.

The 15th is a narrow par 5 hole, measuring less than 500 yards. It offers a roller coaster fairway that is pinched by trees the entire length of the hole. A wonderful risk-reward hole that requires supreme accuracy on every shot. On the day we played I hit a wonderful drive down the center of the fairway. I then hit a 3-iron 210 yards to the left side of the green. My eagle putt slipped by, but I was able to make a nice birdie on this exciting hole.

Another nice touch at Muirfield Village is that Jack hosts a PGA outing in May, called the Memorial Tournament. Each year a great golf contributor is honored and a plaque is created and placed in an outdoor grove. It was fun to finish the round and walk through the grove admiring the plaques of golf's greatest players. Even Jack has his own plague in this hall of fame.

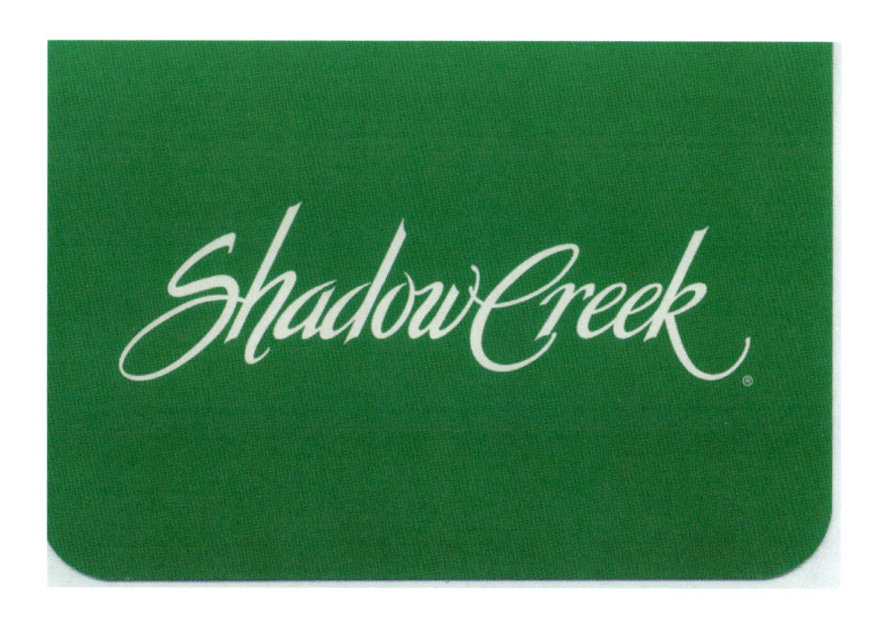

Shadow Creek

In the late 1980's Steve Wynn the owner of many casinos in Las Vegas decided the area needed a great golf course. He hired Tom Fazio and spent $40 million to create a desert oasis that is now Shadow Creek.

When taking the limo from the Bellagio Hotel to Shadow Creek we passed acre after acre of flat, featureless desert land. Arriving at the property gate and driving through the course it was hard to believe this venue was originally that same featureless desert land. Everything within the gates of Shadow Creek was created or transplanted by man. Hills and valleys were shaped, trees were transplanted, water was piped into the complex and even the animals living on the property were imported. It is amazing what can be built by creative people, when money is no object.

Once inside the oasis, you can not see the wastelands beyond the fences, because a large hill was created to encircle the complex, only leaving views of the mountains in the distance. The clubhouse is a moderate one-story white building that is nicely decorated, while the locker room is very spacious. The lockers are adorned with the names of famous celebrities and sports figures who have played the course, including Michael Jordan.

When I first played the course in 1999 it was very difficult to obtain an invitation. Invitations were only provided to "high rollers," who gambled extensively at Mr. Wynn's casinos. Given my personal budgetary constraints I was not one of those high rollers. Funny enough though, I worked for a client in Nashville, Tennessee who turned out to be a high roller. He had previously created and sold a software company and enjoyed gambling, so he visited Vegas 4-5 times a year. After discussing my love of golf, he invited me to join him on one of his trips.

The casinos love high rollers and treat them like kings. In fact Vegas loves them so much, they "comp" the high rollers almost everything for their trip to Vegas. My friend was able to obtain a free room, free food, free shows and free golf during our 3-day stay. I never asked how much he bet, but it was great tagging along for the fun. Now I believe the course is accessible if you stay in one of the Mirage Group hotels and pay $500 dollars.

The enchanting par 3 17th, playing to a green with a waterfall backdrop.

The best hole is the 17th a 150 yard downhill par 3 that plays to the foot of a waterfall. The green is fronted by a lake with the waterfall in the background. What a visional delight. I fortunately hit a nice 9-iron onto the green and escaped with a par.

Some golf purists feel Shadow Creek is an aberration of architecture, given everything is man-made, but I believe it is a creative wonderland that offers a unique golfing experience. One of my favorite inland courses in the world.

The Honors Course

The success of the Coca Cola Company has made a number of men very wealthy. One of those men is Jack Luptin, who founded The Honors Course near Chattanooga, Tennessee.

While living in Atlanta, which is only 2 hours from Chattanooga, I met a work colleague who was an avid golfer and a member of nine different golf clubs. He was not a member of The Honors Course, but one of his business associates was a member. He was kind enough to arrange an outing for me and my family in late November, while they were visiting for Thanksgiving.

The Honors Course allows members to sponsor guests without having to be present. Thus, my father, brother and I were happy recipients of an invitation.

The Honors Course is located in a secluded area and very difficult to find. There are no signs on the roadway or even on the gate to the club. As you approach the gate you push an intercom button and tell the guard your name. By the time you drive from the gate to the club the head professional and caddies are waiting to greet you personally. A very nice touch. They offer you a small guest locker room and access to a snack bar. After changing, we headed for the driving range, then onto the first tee.

The tee shot on the demanding 15th hole at the Honors Course. Notice the dormant Bermuda grass during the Thanksgiving timeframe.

Although The Honors Course is not my favorite Pete Dye design (Casa de Campo in the Dominican Republic is his best work), we did enjoy the golf course. It offers a variety of design styles, switching from links to heath-land from hole to hole. The only design feature I did not like was the massive lake that sits in the middle of the property and comes into play on four holes. It resembled similar lakes Dye has used on other designs and did not seem natural to the area. Otherwise the golf course and the amenities were first class, reflecting Mr. Luptin's grand vision to offer a majestic place to enjoy golf.

Double Eagle

One of the nicest golf course owners you will ever meet is Mr. John McConnell of Columbus, Ohio. Mr. McConnell founded the Double Eagle Club in 1992, asking Tom Weiskopf to design his golf course.

Mr. McConnell hired Tom Weiskopf to create a wonderful golf course that is not only challenging, but fun to play. Weiskopf is one of my favorite architects and this is one of his finest pieces of work. The course provides a full range of holes that require you to play every club in your bag.

My favorite hole is number 17, a 310 yard drivable par 4. The drivable par 4 is a Weiskopf trademark, occurring on every course he designs. The 17th is one of his best. From the tee the golfer has numerous options to play the hole. You can chose to drive the green, which is guarded by a creek on the right, or lay-up to the left leaving a short pitch to the green. On the day we played I tried to drive the green, but pulled my shot left into some trees. I punched out and struggled to make a par. A true risk-reward challenge.

Along with a wonderful routing, the course has the fastest greens I have ever played. They were faster than Augusta (at least when I played) and Oakmont. With the speed of the greens so fast, Weiskopf kept the surfaces fairly flat so the speed would not become too unfair on sloping greens. The flat surfaces became somewhat redundant though, because I seemed to have a straight, fast putt green after green.

I met Mr. Weiskopf on several occasions before playing Double Eagle. He was a guest speaker and golfer at a number of client outings my company sponsored, so I had a chance to spend time on and off the course with him. At one outing we were discussing Double Eagle and he mentioned Mr. McConnell was a very nice man. I then took the opportunity to contact Mr. McConnell and expressed my desire to play his wonderful course and he thankfully agreed to let me play.

After finishing my round at Double Eagle, I noticed Mr. McConnell was having lunch at the club, so I went over to thank him for allowing me to play. We chatted for 20 minutes and he was keenly interested in my assessment of his course, of which I provided a glowing review. A truly nice man who built a truly wonderful course.

The challenging par 4, 5th hole at Double Eagle, offering a scary second shot.

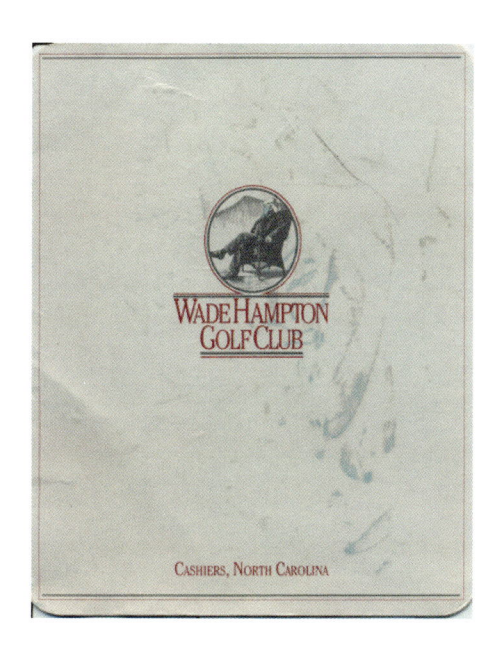

Wade Hampton

In 1990, while living in Atlanta, a number of my golfing friends mentioned a wonderful new course located in Cashiers, North Carolina, which was only 3 hours north of the city. Wade Hampton Golf Club was created by a number of Augusta National members who wanted a place to play while Augusta was closed during the summer. The summers in the mountains of North Carolina are free from soaring temperatures and sticky humidity, making it ideal for golf.

The course was created in 1987 and I learned they were also selling homes along the outskirts of the course. My wife and I had been contemplating purchasing a summer home, so I contacted the real estate agent who covered the Wade Hampton development and expressed an interest in driving to Cashiers to see some homes and possibly play the course. Although the course was very private the main developer of the complex was a member and helped arrange a time for me to play.

Wade Hampton is my favorite Tom Fazio design, along with Shadow Creek. This mountain retreat has a number of spectacular holes, especially the par 3 holes. Two of the par 3's play over a rushing creek that shimmers over large rock formations, causing a cascade effect that is just gorgeous. True to its mountain habitat, there are numerous elevation changes, but you never feel like a goat waking up and down each hill.

My favorite hole is number 3, one of the special par 3's I mentioned above. The hole plays 190 yards, with a green that is tucked next to a fast paced stream that rushes over large boulders to create a waterfall effect that must be cleared to reach the putting surface. A breathtaking natural feature that Fazio used brilliantly.

Although we decided not to purchase a summer house in that area, Wade Hampton remains one of my favorite courses. It is a creative design in a breathtaking part of the United States.

Hidden Gems

There are a number of superb golf courses that are mysteries to most golfers, but always rank highly on Top 100 lists. The main reason for this mystery is the courses are located in remote locations or are extremely private about their existence. This chapter highlights a number of my favorite hidden gems. Even though their locations are remote, these courses are worth the extra plane connection required to hunt them down.

Crystal Downs

As you may have guessed while reading this book, my favorite golf course architect is Alistair Mackenzie, who designed both Augusta National and Cypress Point. While Crystal Downs is not as spectacular as Mackenzie's top two designs, this Michigan beauty is a close third.

During the off-peak seasons (early spring or late fall) Crystal Downs allows non-members to arrange tee times with the head professional. I asked my head professional to call and make a time for me and my friend Gene Greco.

The clubhouse and professional shop resemble an old hunting lodge, giving the club a very rustic feel. The clubhouse sits on a bluff overlooking Lake Michigan, while the professional shop overlooks a smaller lake on the other side called Crystal Lake. The course was built in 1931.

The golf course is pure Mackenzie with undulating greens that have false fronts, large bunkers that possess expansive fingers and wide fairways that allow golfers to play numerous routes to the green. My favorite holes are number 6 and 7. The 6th hole is a 385 yard dogleg to the right, which offers a number of routes to play the hole. A large bunker and tree guard the corner of the dogleg, offering the chance to cut the dogleg or play to the left. The 6th green sits on a tiny knoll, with a number of subtle humps that make putting a real challenge.

The tee shot at number 11, a challenging par 3.

The 7th hole is a 335 yard par 4 that doglegs to the left. After hitting a lay-up short of a hollow, we were faced with a 100 yard pitch to an "L" shaped green that was protected by a huge sand trap on the right and a sharp drop-off on the left. Both holes are challenging and wonderfully strategic.

The weather was warm the day we played. The head pro at the club advised us to take a cart, because the course is quite hilly. We scoffed at using a cart and started our round on foot. The 8th and 9th holes are both severely uphill, really testing our stamina, but at the end of the front nine we were so excited to be playing such a treasure, we did not mind our fatigue. At the 10th hole, we again had an opportunity to grab a motor cart, but decided against the help of modern technology. The back nine was even hillier than the front, which really wore us down. By the time we reached the 18th green we could barely make it to the clubhouse for a much needed refreshment. Although we were tired, we enjoyed every step on this Midwest jewel.

Prairie Dunes

No offense to my friends from this great state, but now you have a good reason to visit the heartland of Kansas. Hutchinson, Kansas to be specific. The nearest airport to Hutchinson is in Wichita, about 2 hours away. The reason to visit the "Land of Oz" is to play a spectacular course called Prairie Dunes.

Prairie Dunes is a wonderful links style course calling itself "A touch of Scotland in Kansas." This saying is truly accurate, because the course has been carved from grassy sand dunes, which are now covered with Yucca bushes and scrub. One would swear they were playing a course near Edinburgh.

During the work week Prairie Dunes allows reciprocal privileges to members of other private clubs. Thus, I asked my head professional to contact their head pro to arrange a time for me to play. I was working in Dallas at the time, so it was easy to book a commuter flight to Wichita.

Although the entire course is memorable, the front nine is where the most spectacular holes lay, especially the par 3 holes. Holes number 2 and 4 are wonderful par 3's, both playing around 165 yards. They both play to a plateau green that is set into a sand dune and fronted by gapping bunkers.

The other special hole on the front nine is number 8, a 435 par 4 that doglegs to the right and plays slightly uphill. The emerald green fairway is carved through the deep amber prairie grass that frames the hole. After hitting a decent drive I hit a good medium iron towards the green, only to see it drop short into a massive sand trap. I executed a nice trap shot, but 2 putted for a disappointing bogey.

The best hole on the back nine is another par 3, number 10, a 185-yarder playing over a wasteland to a green perched on a small hill. This was another wonderful single shot hole that typified the ruggedly beautiful terrain of this special area.

Camargo

Unlike the remote locations of Crystal Downs and Prairie Dunes, the Camargo Club is actually located in a city that is easily accessible from all points in America. Camargo is located in a sleepy suburb of Cincinnati, Ohio. The club is very private though and not many people have heard about this Midwestern Gem.

The club is reported to have an older membership, making it difficult to meet a member, even in the business world. I was able to access the club by playing in a US Amateur tournament qualifying event. Each year before the golf season starts, I review the list of courses used by the United States Golf Association (USGA) for amateur event regional qualifying. Camargo was the site of the Amateur qualifying for southern Ohio, so I wrote the USGA requesting to move my qualifying site from my home town to Cincinnati, because I was doing extensive work in the city at that time. The USGA agreed and allowed me to qualify at Camargo.

Although I failed to qualify for the national event, I really enjoyed playing such a unique venue. The architect for Camargo is Seth Raynor who built the course in 1921. Having played a number of other Raynor designs, including Shore Acres in Chicago and the National Golf Links, I recognized many of his distinctive features at Camargo. The greens are large and undulating, with a number of them sitting on a slight plateau. The driving areas are wide and receptive, bordered by long, thick grass. The course was a delight to play, even though I hit more shots than I wanted.

Kittansett

This is another gem that is not as remote as some clubs, but still an effort to find. The Kittansett Club is located in Marion, Massachusetts about 90 minutes south of Boston or one hour north of Providence. The club is situated on a point that juts into Buzzards Bay, near Cape Cod.

During the off-season (late Fall or early Spring) the club allows reciprocal play with other private clubs.

The club reeks of New England values, having a rustic clubhouse that resembles a beach cottage, with graying wood slates and a wood shingled roof. The accommodations were very simple and functional.

The golf course is not overly demanding, unless the wind is howling. It offers a variety of wide open holes and those carved from the short pine trees that dot the course.

The best hole at Kittansett and maybe in all of New England is number 3, a 175 yard par 3 that is played on the beach. Yes, that is correct, the tee and the green lie on a beach next to Buzzards Bay. The green sits like an emerald perched above the white sandy beach. This is truly a unique hole that seems to naturally blend into its surroundings. After playing the hole I still could not determine whether the architect or Mother Nature had been the designer. A true compliment to the architect.

My son Cooper standing on the isolated 3rd hole green at Kittansett, which juts into Buzzards Bay

The Valley Club of Montecito

Two hours northwest of the traffic and congestion of Los Angeles is the city of Santa Barbara. A college town that is also a haven for the rich. Montecito is a small town on the outskirts of Santa Barbara, that is home to another wonderful Alistair Mackenzie designed golf course.

The Valley Club of Montecito was built in 1929 and is one of Mackenzie's top five designs. The course embodies many of his design philosophies and is reminiscent of his design at Pasatiempo; especially the way he used an arroyo to toughen the driving areas of most holes. The Valley Club is more of a shot maker's course than his other designs, requiring more accuracy from the tee. Many of the holes dogleg slightly requiring the player to shape his shots to fit the hole.

The Valley Club has a local membership that is quite exclusive. During my consulting days in Los Angeles I worked with a client in San Diego who had played the Valley Club with a member friend. My client and I played a number of rounds together and he asked if I would like to play the Valley Club. I said yes, and he arranged for us to play with his member friend.

My favorite hole at the Valley Club is number 15, a long par 4 that doglegs to the right. The green is situated directly in front of the stately white stucco clubhouse, surrounded by large Mackenzie bunkers. Playing the approach shot to the green offers a beautifully broad visual that includes the elegant clubhouse.

The Valley Club is very private, but if you can find a member to play, it is worth the long drive from Los Angeles.

My favorite hole at the Valley Club, the spacious 15th hole playing to a green set close to the stunning clubhouse.

Eugene Country Club

Eugene Country Club has one of the best and friendliest head golf professionals in all of golf. He has been the head professional for ten years and has already become an asset to the club. Of course I am a bit biased, because the head pro at Eugene is my brother Mark.

Located two hours south of Portland, Eugene is a college town that is home to the Fighting Ducks of the University of Oregon. My brother played golf for the University and became an All-American while playing for the Ducks.

The club allows reciprocal play from other private clubs, so have your professional contact my brother to arrange a game. It will be worth your time, especially if you are on your way to play Bandon or Pacific Dunes.

The course was originally designed by Chandler Egan in 1923, but in 1967 Robert Trent Jones was hired to do a complete redesign. Trent Jones literally turned the course on its head, by reversing many of the holes, putting tees where greens were and greens where tees once existed. Today the course is a beautiful parkland venue, with wonderfully enormous fir trees towering on every hole. The best holes are the par 3's, all of which play across water to large undulating greens.

If you have a chance to venture to the Pacific Northwest, take time to play Eugene. Not only is the head pro a great guy, but the course is one of the most beautiful places in America.

My brother Mark, the head professional, and my son Cooper, standing on the 5th green of the Eugene Country Club

Forest Highlands

Although Flagstaff, Arizona is only 2-3 hours from the Valley of the Sun in Phoenix, it is a world apart in climate and fauna. Flagstaff is located in the northwest part of Arizona, which is near the Sierra Nevada Mountain range. The climate is much cooler in both the summer and the winter, offering a high plains feel, with thick forests of pine trees, similar to the environment at Castle Pines Golf Club near Denver.

Forest Highlands is another top course that offers reciprocal privileges to members of other private clubs, but only in the off-season (early spring or late fall). This is a fine Tom Weiskopf design, carved from a rich forest of pines. The course offers numerous water hazards and of course a drivable par 4. Some of the views of distant mountains are breathtaking.

The demanding tee shot on number 9, a majestic par 4 that includes a stream, lake and massive bunkers.

My favorite hole is number 9, a long par 4 hole, measuring 455 yards. The tee shot starts from a high ridge above the fairway, with the approach shot needing to avoid a large lake on the right and a cliff on the left. A picturesque setting that you will not forget.

If the golf course does not offer you enough incentive to make the trek to Flagstaff, then consider the route from Phoenix takes you through Sedona, Arizona. Sedona is a desert paradise encircled by a natural cathedral of cliffs and large rock outcroppings. The cliffs are intensely colorful, contrasted by the blue sky and the brown desert. A wonderfully tranquil drive towards a rewarding top 100 course.

Black Diamond Ranch

It may be odd to consider a golf course in Florida to be a "hidden gem," but the Black Diamond Ranch Country Club in Lecanto is a true "Diamond in the Rough." Located 2 hours Northwest of Orlando, Black Diamond Ranch looks like a course built in New York or New Jersey. The terrain is very unique to Florida, offering rolling hills and a variety of trees.

Along with the unique topography the course also has a wonderful old quarry that comes into play on five back-nine holes. The quarry creates a spectacular backdrop, offering a "granite curtain" that provides a marvelous silhouette framing the holes.

Of the five holes that traverse the quarry, number 15 is particularly spectacular. The hole measures 371 yards and starts with a tee perched on the rim of the quarry. The hole then falls to the quarry floor and is flanked by a large lake on the left, which hugs the large green. Bunkers are artfully placed throughout the hole to offer both guidance and hazards for wayward shots.

Holes number 14 and 16 play along the quarry ridge, above the 15th, offering wonderful cliffside golf that is both challenging and beautiful. The other two holes, 13 and 17 are picturesque par 3's that play through the quarry.

The Quarry Course at Black Diamond Ranch was built in 1988 by Tom Fazio, as part of a large residential community. I gained access by contacting the membership chairman in the early 1990's to inquire about joining the club. Being a new course, they were eager to host me for a round of golf to showoff the community and amenities. It is a nice Florida location that offers unique golf in a state filled with a variety of courses.

Public Pearls

Unlike the other courses discussed in this book, the golf tracks in this section are public access venues, although most are extremely expensive. Gaining access to these public pearls is just a matter of planning and persistence. Some require a stay in their adjoining resort hotel to obtain an advanced tee time, but everyone is invited to play.

I encourage all golfers, who enjoy traveling and playing the best courses, to take time to explore these treasures. The cost is sometimes high, but the reward is even greater. Other fabulous public destinations, I do not discuss in this section, but should be on your must play list are Bandon Dunes in Oregon, the Kiawah Ocean Course in South Carolina and the Cascades course in Virginia.

Pebble Beach

Preparing to hit my tee-shot from the 18th tee at Pebble Beach, with the surf crashing into the boulders that guard the fairway and the wind rushing off the ocean, was one of the most exhilarating single moments in my golfing life. There is no finer finishing hole in golf.

The 18th is just one of many fine holes at Pebble Beach. Pebble has nine holes bordering the ocean, more than any top course in the world. The stretch of holes from #4 through #10 is probably the most beautiful continuous stretch of seven golf holes in the world.

Along with St Andrews in Scotland, Pebble is the most famous public access venue in the world. Even non-golfers have heard of Pebble Beach, because of its' astounding beauty and golfing history.

My wife Lissa resting before we attack the demanding second shot on number 8, one of the best approach shots in golf.

Along with the 18th, I have a number of favorite holes. Number 7, measuring a slight 110 yards, is a wonderful downhill par 3 that can play very difficult if the wind is blowing. The small green is completely surrounded by sand and sits near the edge of the cliffs. We all hear stories about professionals hitting 3-iron into the gale, but that is very hard to believe after playing the hole. For a decent golfer a punch 7-iron may be the strongest club they would hit.

The 8th is also a very special hole, offering one of the great approach shots in the world. The view from the tee is a bit disappointing, because it is blind to the fairway. You aim into the horizon and guess where to hit your ball. Once on top of the plateau you face an extremely difficult second shot to a small green that seems to be floating out over the edge of the cliff. I have played Pebble 5 times and never hit the green, almost always pulling it left into the bunkers or leaving it short in the fairway.

The 17th is also one of my favorites. Many memorable shots have been played at this hole during professional tournaments. Nicklaus hitting the flagstick with his 1-iron tee shot in the 1972 US Open and Tom Watson chipping in from the left rough to seal his US Open victory, over Nicklaus in 1982.

The distinctive architectural features at Pebble are the small greens and deep greenside bunkers. The greens are much smaller than those built today, almost half their size, making them hard to hit from the fairway. They are also overgrown with Po-Ana, which is a weed-type grass that is very aggressive and grows well near the ocean. Po-Ana greens are sometimes difficult to putt, because they do not remain consistently smooth throughout the day.

Although Pebble is one of the most expensive courses in the world (over $400 per person) it is worth saving your pennies for at least one round. You will be thankful for the experience.

Finishing a wonderful round at Pebble Beach on the best 18th hole in the world.

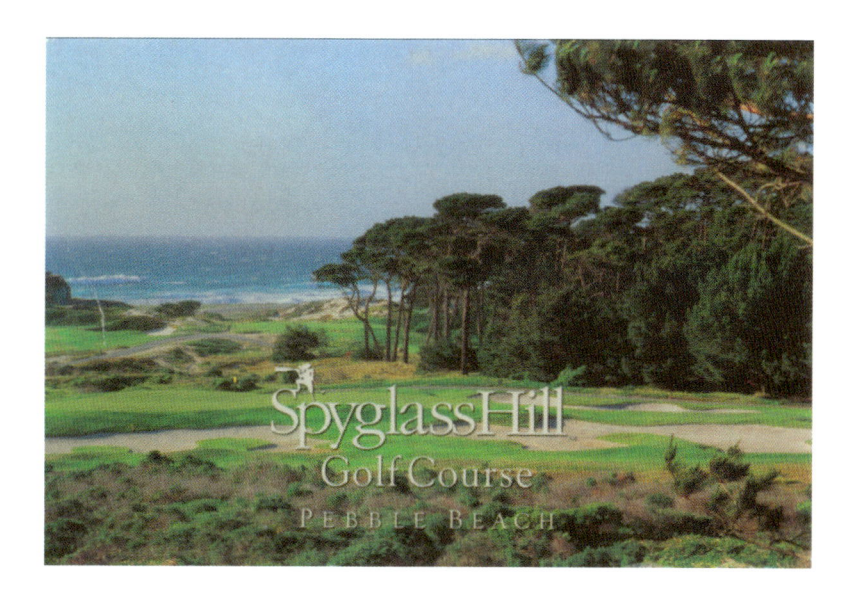

Spyglass Hill

Less than two miles from Pebble Beach lays Spyglass Hill Golf Club. Spyglass is my favorite Robert Trent Jones design, because it offers a truly unique start to a memorable course.

The first five holes at Spyglass play through exposed sand dunes. The emerald green blots dot the pearl white sand, creating a wonderfully colorful and beautiful canvas.

The first green is completely surrounded by sand and is difficult to hit, given the near 600 yards traveled from the tee. The second hole is a short par 4 that plays from an island fairway to a green perched at the top of a large dune.

The third and fourth holes are truly spectacular. The 3rd is a 150 yard par 3 that plays from near the 2nd green to a small "L" shaped green that sits well below the tee. The view from the 3rd tee towards the ocean is wonderful. The green is completely swallowed by sandy dunes and ice-plant covered hills. When the wind is blowing from off the ocean, the hole can play very difficult.

The 4th hole is one of the best holes in golf. It is a twisting dogleg left, par 4 that measures only 365 yards long. Sand dunes engulf the fairway and the green along the entire length of the hole. The most fascinating aspect of the hole is the snake-like green that is cradled into a small sand dune basin. When you arrive at the green, the sand dunes are almost eye-level, which gives the green a submerged feel. What a wonderful use of the natural surroundings.

My son Cooper playing a difficult sand shot from the dunes near the 3rd green at Spyglass.

The 5th hole is another nice par 3 that plays from one dune to another, finishing a memorable stretch of golf holes carved from the sand dunes. The 6th is the start of the 'rest of the course" at Spyglass. The remaining 13 holes at Spyglass are very nice, but do not match the majesty of the first 5 holes. In fact, if Spyglass possessed three or four more dune holes, it would probably rank in the top 20, instead of the top 50 courses in America.

Like Pebble, Spyglass is expensive ($285 per person), but worth at least one round. It makes the trip to the Monterey Peninsula one of the best on earth.

Pinehurst #2

Like Pebble Beach, Pinehurst is now an official member of the US Open rotation. Pinehurst first hosted the prestigious championship in 1999, won by Payne Stewart and again in 2005 won by Michael Campbell.

Pinehurst is another nice Donald Ross design, but is not as memorable as other more beautiful courses. We often hear that Pinehurst offers subtle architectural features, which in my definition means it is not spectacular, but does offer a fine venue for testing your skills.

When asked about my favorite hole at Pinehurst, it is difficult to differentiate the entire 18 holes. This tells me that, like many Ross designs, the course is very balanced, with few real stars. The fifth hole is very nice, offering a wonderfully difficult approach shot to a bunkered green from a sloping fairway. The greens at Pinehurst are like inverted saucers, with wonderful collection areas surrounding each green. From the fairway the greens look rather large, but when you arrive at the green site, you see 20-30% of the surface slopes off to the sides, making the target much smaller than originally thought.

The course is carved from a forest of southern pines, with sandy outlying areas, covered with pine straw, encasing every hole. The terrain is rolling, but not too hilly, making it an enjoyable course to walk. Although trees border every hole, they really do not come into play, because the fairway corridors are very wide.

TPC Sawgrass

How can such a short par 3-hole strike fear into so many golfers? Of course I am speaking about the treacherous 17th hole at the Tournament Players Course (TPC) at Sawgrass.

The 17th hole measures 140 yards from the back tee, but plays to an island green, which sits near the middle of a pond. In 1980 when the hole was built by architect Pete Dye, it was a creative novelty that instantly provided the TPC at Sawgrass with exposure and fanfare for its' unique design.

I have played the tiny hole 4 times and have always found the green, which is quite an accomplishment given the number of professionals that find the water each year during the Tournament Players Championship. Although the 17th is wonderful, the TPC at Sawgrass is much more than a one-hole course. The finishing holes of 16, 17 and 18 make up one of the most difficult and exciting finishes in championship golf. During the tournament players can make anything from a one to an eight in this stretch of wonderful holes.

Although the novelty of Dye's design has worn off through the years, this is still a great place to play golf. The course is kept in tournament condition almost year-around, so it is fun to play the same track the professionals play to test your skills.

Blackwolf Run- River Course

One hour north of Milwaukee lay one of the most impressive public golf facilities in the world. Kohler, Wisconsin is home to four wonderful courses, all owned by Herb Kohler, of bathroom fixture fame. Mr. Kohler hired Pete Dye to build four unique courses that are all worthy of hosting professional championships. In fact his Whistling Straits course will host the 2005 PGA Championship, while the two courses at Blackwolf Run were used to host the 1996 Women's US Open.

My favorite of the bunch is the River Course at Blackwolf Run. Here Pete Dye masterfully utilized the Sheboygan River to create entertaining holes that are unique in the world of golf. The entire back nine of the River Course is spectacular, as holes border and traverse the flowing body of water.

During my first trip to Blackwolf Run the salmon were spawning and the river was full of fish fighting their way upstream. We would hear them flapping furiously against the rushing stream as we played shots on the back nine. Dye routed many of the holes around bends of the river, which require the golfer to make choices to be heroic and hit directly over the river, or play safe and avoid the watery temptations.

The course is very difficult, but fair. Long summer grass borders all fairways, which are wide at the right places to accept miss-hits when they occur. The greens have character and offer perfectly manicured putting surfaces. A wonderful and beautiful test.

I prefer the River Course to Whistling Straits, because the River Course looks very natural in a gorgeous setting. The Whistling Straits course looks a bit contrived, which it was, given the property was originally a flat airfield that Dye needed to spruce up. Whistling Straits has a number of poor holes that look out-of-place, especially the 18th hole, which forces the player to hit the tee shoe straight uphill to a small landing area and then traverse a gully to the green. I am also not a fan of Dye's use of large ledges in his fairways, which look out-of-place on a links layout.

Even though Whistling Straits has some design flaws the views of Lake Michigan are incredible and a number of holes are quite fun to play. The quartet of courses offers a fantastic golfing destination for all golf lovers.

Playing the spectacular par 3, 13th at Blackwolf Run with my friend Tom McCleary.

Mauna Kea

Mauna Kea Golf Course, located on the Big Island of Hawaii, was the 100th course I played to complete my Quest. It is an entertaining course that is fun to play, especially if you have kids who enjoy the game.

Lucky for me, my family was able to join me for the final chapter of my American Quest. Like most courses in Hawaii, it is beautiful and well maintained.

There is only one hole that plays on the ocean, which is the 4th hole, a spectacular 210 yard par 3, which plays over a small inlet to a large green. It offers a similar visual and entertaining experience to the 16th at Cypress Point. The day we played I decided to play the tournament tees of the course. The wind was light, so I hit a strong 4-iron, which barely cleared the cliffs and rolled next to the pin. I missed the putt, but was satisfied with par.

Any trip to Hawaii is nice, especially if you can play golf. The Mauna Kea course is very enjoyable and holds a special place in my heart, so I highly recommend playing this Pacific jewel.

Completing my Quest with the ones I love most, my daughter Cara and son Cooper, with my wife Lissa taking this historic picture at the memorable 4th hole at Mauna Kea, my 100th Top 100 Course.

Toughest Ticket in Town

As mentioned in the first chapter of the book, accomplishing my quest was a test in personal networking and persistence. I was very fortunate to have gained access to so many private bastions of golf.

Below I have ranked the five toughest golf clubs in the Top 100 to access, in my humble opinion. Other courses may actually be tougher to access, but in my journey, these proved to be the most challenging.

They all have similar characteristics related to gaining entry:

    a. Guests much play with a member
    b. Memberships are small in number
    c. Club is very private
    d. Golf Professional network is not helpful
    e. Rarely, if ever, open the course to charity or open tournaments

These characteristics are a tough combination of attributes to crack, although given my own experience, it can be done.

1. **Augusta National** --- Playing Augusta National is the last step to heaven for most golf lovers. The membership is fiercely private and obtaining an invitation is a rare occurrence. In fact many of the members live across the country, which means they have to make special plans to play, including hotels, cars, etc, which makes the playing process that much more difficult. The course is also closed in the summer, eliminating nearly four months of play each year. All golfers want a shot at this titan, and the members are aware of the unique gate key they hold, so are careful about who is invited. The membership is composed of business leaders across the country, so if you do business with one of these corporate titans you may be able to make arrangements to play.

2. **The Country Club** --- Unless you get married and hold your reception at The Country Club, like I did, gaining access to this venerable old club in New England is nearly impossible. On a trip to Boston, before meeting my wife, my head professional called The Country Club to arrange a game for me to play and the club laughed at his request. Thus, find a nice New England girl living in Boston with the right connections and get married at The Country Club. It worked for me. My perception is that many of the members are prominent doctors and lawyers, so the next time you visit your physician, ask them about their golf network.

3. **Los Angeles Country Club** – Right on the outskirts of Beverly Hills sits one of golf's most private and exclusive golf clubs. This club is so exclusive it rarely extends membership invitations to people involved in the entertainment business,

which is quite a crowd to exclude with Hollywood so near. The membership seems to be filled with lawyers and other professionals living in Southern California.

4. **Chicago Golf Club** --- When I played, the average age of the membership at Chicago Golf Club was almost 70 years old. Thus it was difficult for people in their 30's and 40's to find access to members. The club has started to admit younger members, but it is still difficult to find an access point.

5. **The Golf Club** --- It has a small, all-men's membership that is serious about playing good golf on a strong championship course. The club seems to be composed of Ohio based business men, ranging from auto dealership owners to professionals in the services business, such as auditing or legal services. If you work for a company that utilizes one of the large Audit firms, ask the partner who handles your account about accessing the course.

My Top 10 Favorite Courses

Each rating organization has a specific criteria for deciding the top 100 courses in America and in the World. The criteria is fairly similar across organizations, focusing on course quality, the overall experience, resistance to scoring, the aesthetics, grooming, along with other more specific measures. I agree with these metrics, but weight mine slightly differently, focusing more on memorability and architectural quality, along with the overall impact of the experience. I am less interested in the resistance to scoring or grooming characteristics of a course.

Listed below are the courses I want to play again and again. Many of the top championship courses, which are not on my list, focus on resistance to scoring as their trademark, which is less interesting to me. I prefer a fun round on a challenging course, which is extremely beautiful or offers unique characteristics. That is not to say I do not appreciate a stern test, because you will find championship courses on my list, but these championship courses are the ones that offer a tough test, wrapped in a stunning experience.

One of my best tests of golf course greatness is whether I can remember every hole once I have finished the round. These courses meet that standard for greatness. Try this test at the next top course you play and you will be surprised how difficult it is to distinguish the holes, unless the course is unique and well balanced.

1. **Cypress Point** --- The most beautiful and well balanced course in the world. Cypress is not long nor difficult, but is a pure pleasure to play. The aesthetics are off the scale and the finishing holes are like walking through heaven to reach the "pearly gates." A breathtaking masterpiece, designed by the most ingenious architect of all-time.

2. **Pebble Beach** --- The best public venue in the world, having nine cliff-side holes, which separates this course from all the others. Nothing can match playing on seaside cliffs during a warm spring day, with seals barking away and the sea-spray bathing the shimmering fairways. Fun to play, but very demanding when the wind is blowing.

3. **Pine Valley** --- Always ranked number one by almost all rating organizations, Pine Valley is like no other course in the world. One of the rare courses, that is extremely demanding, but offers incredible aesthetics, making the round a pure pleasure to play.

4. **Oakmont** --- Offers the richest history and heritage of any club in America. The golf course is very penal, but unique. They have recently eliminated thousands of trees, which will help bring the course back to the original design.

5. **Augusta National** --- The total package experience at Augusta is unlike any other in golf. With a deep history and a number of very special holes, it offers a mystical aura that is unrivaled in golf. The front nine is mediocre, but the back nine is a shining star. A sacred location, where you can mingle with the spirit of golfing gods

6. **Seminole** --- My favorite Donald Ross course, combining beauty with strategic golf. The unkempt look and ocean-side setting create a masterpiece on the Atlantic coast.

7. **Shinnecock Hills** --- America's best links course, it has just enough wonderful holes to counter the brutal conditions that exist if the wind is blowing hard.

8. **Prairie Dunes** --- An enjoyable family oriented club in the "Land of Oz." You really believe you are in Scotland while playing. The collection of par 3's may be the best in America.

9. **Merion** --- Although short and stuffed into a small piece of property, this course has so many excellent holes I had to add it to my list. The history is unparalled, letting you walk the path of Bobby Jones, Jack Nicklaus and Ben Hogan.

10. **National Golf Links** --- Unlike its neighbor Shinnecock, this course is fun to play and offers a real old-world feel. A throw-back to the early days of golf architecture.

"This is the exact book educators and students need to comprehensively understand the current state of the global fashion business. Future industry professionals will now be well equipped to take on the challenges of international retailing, marketing and merchandising."
Michelle Childs, Associate Professor, Retail and Merchandising Management, The University of Tennessee, USA

"A very comprehensive text, which makes a positive contribution to the subject knowledge of fashion business, offering a truly global viewpoint."
Ruth Marciniak, Programme Leader MSC Fashion and Lifestyle Marketing, Glasgow Caledonian University, UK

In *Global Fashion Business*, Dr. Byoungho Ellie Jin guides you through the challenges of expanding your fashion brand internationally. With examples from large and small companies, developing and developed countries, and online and offline retailers, you'll discover strategies to overcome economic, cultural, legal, and regulatory obstacles. You'll also gain practical insights for country-specific marketing and retailing, from market selection to pricing—making this your essential tool for success in the global fashion marketplace.

BYOUNGHO ELLIE JIN is the Albert Myers Distinguished Professor in the Department of Textile and Apparel, Technology and Management at North Carolina State University, USA. Her contribution to the global fashion marketing and branding discipline can be found in more than 140 journal articles and numerous funded research projects. She is the co-author of *Fashion Business* (2002) as well as *Brands Rule the World* (2015), and co-editor of *Fashion Brand Internationalization* (2016), *Fashion Branding and Communication* (2017) and *Process Innovation in the Global Fashion Industry* (2019). Dr. Jin served as president of the International Textile and Apparel Association (ITAA) in 2021.

PowerPoint slides outlining a suggested course structure and class notes are available at:
https://bloomsbury.pub/global-fashion-business

FASHION

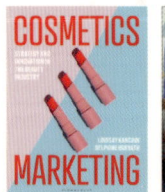

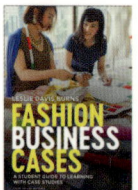

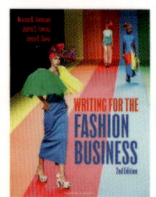

BLOOMSBURY VISUAL ARTS

Cover design by Holly Cap
Cover images © andersphoto and WinWin/Adobe St

Also available from Bloomsbury Visual Arts
www.bloomsbury.com

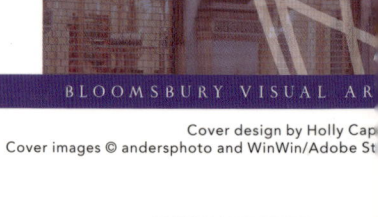

ISBN 978-1-350-18018-5

My 5 Favorite Golf Architects

Golf course architecture is an art form, similar to painting or designing buildings. Picking my favorites is like trying to decide between Monet, Picasso or Renoir. Each artist has his own style and design philosophy. While the painter has a canvas, the golf course architect has landscape and topography. The architect must utilize the property he is given, consider the wind, leverage natural features such as streams, creeks, boulders, and factor in sunlight and how the course will play at different times of the year. The architect is also bound by the wishes of the property owner, who may desire a particular type of course on his land.

While I enjoy many architectural art forms, the five architects listed below are my favorites. I have not played all their creations, but have really enjoyed the ones I have played. The key similarity between the five is they all have created unique golfing experiences that are vividly memorable. Their designs are in perfect harmony with the canvas they were provided. If one of their creations is near you, public or private, make time to play their works of art.

1. **Alistair Mackenzie** --- Every Mackenzie course I have played has been artfully designed and fun to play. Mackenzie was a master tactician, who wanted to provide courses that challenge the professional, while allowing the beginner to enjoy the round. Mackenzie is famous for epitomizing the "Strategic" design philosophy, requiring golfers to consider many options, while playing a hole. His work at Cypress Point, Augusta National, Pasatiempo, the Valley Club of Montecito and Crystal Downs is heavenly.

2. **CB Macdonald & Seth Raynor** --- I am a big fan of links golf in Scotland and Ireland, so any course that offers this style of architecture becomes a favorite. CB Macdonald and Seth Raynor created classic links style courses that mixed old favorite holes from Scotland, with new concoctions in America. Macdonald and Raynor collaborated on the National Golf Links and Chicago Golf Club, while Raynor also created Camargo, Shore Acres and a number of other highly touted courses on his own. Their designs are truly unique and time-tested.

3. **Tom Weiskopf** ---- Not all his creations are spectacular, but most are very enjoyable and well balanced. Weiskopf offers a variety of options on most holes, particularly his drivable par 4's and his reachable par 5's. His desert creations at Troon and Troon North, along with his work at Forest Highlands, Double Eagle and Loch Lomond in Scotland are all very impressive. I have never finished one of his courses, without being extremely pleased.

4. **AW Tillinghast** --- Tillinghast did a wide range of courses, offering difficult, penal designs like Winged Foot West and Bethpage, while creating delicate enjoyable courses like Somerset Hills and Baltimore Country Club. I tend to favor his milder designs, because they are more enjoyable and usually more visual appeal.

A Tillinghast gem, the 11th at Quaker Ridge, a short, but deadly par 4.

5. **Ben Crenshaw & Bill Coore** --- This dynamic duo has created some real masterpieces recently. Their work at Sand Hills in Nebraska is spectacular and their other designs, like Cuscowilla in Georgia, are creatively entertaining. Crenshaw and Coore are known for their "minimalist" design philosophy, which means they utilize the natural features of the property, without adding many man-made elements. I understand their work at the Friar's Club on Long Island is spectacular and will add to their fame.

Along with these favorites, a number of other architects have created wonderful courses through the years. I like the work of architects from the 1920's and 1930's, including Willie Watson, William Flynn and Perry Maxwell. I also like some of the courses designed by Donald Ross, but most of his are very conservative and not overly memorable, except his work at Seminole.

A few modern-day architects have also created some exciting tracks. I have enjoyed a number of intriguing layouts created by Jack Nicklaus and Pete Dye. Both have distinctive styles, but I enjoy their "softer" efforts, like Muirfield Village and Blackwolf Run. I also enjoy the minimalist work of Tom Doak, who did a wonderful job routing the course at Pacific Dunes. I have also played a number of Tom Fazio designs that are enjoyable, like Wade Hampton and Shadow Creek, but even these special tracks have been tarnished by his over-use of bunkering.

The Best 18 Holes in America

After playing the best courses in America, I thought it would be fun to "design" my dream golf course. Thus, I have picked the best 18 holes in America from the top 100 courses on my list.

The parameters and criteria I used to pick the top 18 is a bit unique, but here is my rationale:

1. Pick the Best Hole by Number --- I believe the positioning of a hole, within the body of an 18-hole course, is important, because great holes fit like a jigsaw puzzle at each course to create the grand mosaic designed by the architect. Thus, I picked the best number one hole, best number two hole, and so on, which is much harder than just picking 18 random holes.

2. Only One Hole per Course ---- I also added a bit of sophistication and challenge by only allowing myself to pick one hole per course. This way my dream 18 takes me across the country, instead of picking the three holes and Amen Corner, or the three holes at Cypress Point.

3. Create a Balanced Dream 18 --- Another challenging aspect I dictated was to pick a "real looking" course from a scorecard perspective. As you will see my dream 18 has four par 3's, four par 5's and holes with a variety of length and difficulty. As people say, "Variety is the Spice of Life," and this course is very spicy.

4. Aesthetics & Memorability are the Key --- As noted throughout this book, I enjoy courses and golf holes that are unique, memorable and beautiful. These characteristics are evident in the holes I have chosen.

When dreaming about my heavenly 18, I sit back and try to envision playing each hole and then "beaming" to the next location to play the next hole. I hope you enjoy the journey as well. Also, try to pick your own Dream 18 using similar rules. It is harder than you think.

My Dream 18
Official Scorecard

Hole #	Course	Par	Yardage
1	Merion	4	360
2	Peachtree	5	525
3	Ocean Course at Kiawah	4	390
4	Spyglass Hill	4	365
5	Eugene	3	185
6	Seminole	4	385
7	San Francisco	3	170
8	Prairie Dunes	4	435
9	Oakmont	5	495
	Total Out	36	3310
10	Pine Valley	3	145
11	Pasatiempo	4	390
12	Southern Hills	4	455
13	Augusta National	5	505
14	Shinnecock Hills	4	445
15	Black Diamond Ranch	4	371
16	Cypress Point	3	233
17	National Golf Links	4	385
18	Pebble Beach	5	545
	Total In	36	3474
Total 18		72	6784

As you can see by the scorecard, my Dream Course is not extremely long. The course reflects my preference for well conceived holes that are memorable, beautiful and most of all unique, while still providing a fair challenge. The location of the holes covers all regions of the United States, from the Pacific Coast through the Great Plains, past the Great Lakes area, to the shores of the Atlantic. When will "Scotty build a transporter" to beam us directly to each course, so that my Dream Round can become reality?

Merion #1

Like Alistair Mackenzie, I believe the first hole should not be too difficult, allowing the player to initiate a good start. The first at Merion is neither too long nor difficult and has an added bonus of being situated directly in front of their marvelous clubhouse. A wonderful setting to start my Dream 18.

Peachtree #2

I love risk-reward designed holes and number 2 at Peachtree in Atlanta is a real beauty. The drive must be well struck to reach the crest of a hill to allow options for hitting the second shot. You can shoot for the green on your second shot or lay-up in two different areas of the fairway. A lake splits the fairway in two, and extends to the right side of the green. The second shot is downhill, presenting an enchanting view of danger and beauty. Once you arrive at the green the fun really starts, because the members tell me "an elephant has been buried there." A huge mound in the middle of the green challenges all putts.

Ocean #3

This hole is short, but devilish. A real favorite of architect Pete Dye, who created this bewitching masterpiece. The hole normally plays downwind, which makes holding the platform green that much harder. After hitting a 220 yard shot to the middle of the fairway, the player is faced with an exacting approach to a green that is raised 4-5 feet above the fairway. It literally looks like a small billiards table that is impossible to hit.

Spyglass #4   The first five holes at Spyglass Hill are heavenly and number 4 is the best of the lot. The hole resembles a green serpent curving to the left through impressive white sand dunes covered in ice plant. The green is somewhat submerged into a large dune, creating a mini-amphitheatre around a long, skinny green.

Spyglass #4

120

Eugene #5 — This beautiful par 3 plays downhill across a small lake to a large green that is framed with huge Douglas Fir trees. It epitomizes golf in the Pacific Northwest, displaying a rugged beauty and charm.

Eugene #5

Seminole #6 — Ben Hogan called #6 one of the best par 4's in the country. It is a strategic gem that plays between bushes on the right and huge sand traps on the left. An exacting hole that requires accuracy over brawn.

San Francisco #7 — One of the prettiest par 3 holes in the world. The "Dual Hole" is a downhill hole set in a natural canyon, with an undulating green surrounded by bunkers.

Prairie Dunes #8 — Exemplifies the rugged unkempt beauty of this Heartland masterpiece. The hole plays uphill, doglegging to the right around fields of long, brown prairie grass. Massive sandy waste areas help frame this hole, which is probably the toughest on my Dream front-nine.

Oakmont #9 — My Dream 18 needed a practice putting green, so it is fitting that I include this unique hole, which doubles for the putting green at Oakmont. Number 9 is also a short par 5 that can yield eagles and birdies, making the round more enjoyable.

Pine Valley #10 — The 10th at Pine Valley poses a table-top green set above unkempt waste areas, which surround the putting surface. A deep pot bunker guards the right front portion of the green, collecting thin shots that were not properly struck. A short, but nasty hole that requires precision and guts.

Pasatiempo #11 — This medium length par 4 is bisected by a deep arroyo, which runs the entire length of the hole. The drive must stay right and short of the ditch, while the green sits precariously on the far left edge of the arroyo. Although the yardage is not long the hole plays uphill, making the second shot very demanding to a small green. Another strategic masterpiece by Alistair Mackenzie.

Pasatiempo #11

Southern Hills #12

Although Southern Hills is not one of my favorite courses (it is too hard), the 12th is a lovely hole that requires both strength and accuracy. The hole plays uphill for the first 300 yards and then presents a tough approach shot over a small lake. If you do not hit a long, accurate drive, in the fairway, you must lay-up your approach shot.

Augusta National #13

One of the most strategic holes in the world. This short par 5 offers an abundance of options for golfers of all levels. It offers danger and great rewards, which is especially wonderful during a tight Masters Tournament. Players can eagle the hole or make double bogey, creating a forum for elation or disaster. An exciting hole that gets your adrenaline pumping.

Shinnecock Hills #14

A tough par 4 hole that plays slightly uphill. The setting is quite spectacular as the hole is carved from long, brown sea-grass and ancient sand hills. The green sits in a small hollow, surrounded by bushes and sandy waste area.

Black Diamond Ranch #15

A stunning hole set in the floor of an abandoned quarry. The tee shot starts on the rim of the quarry, shooting down onto the quarry floor, before finishing at a green set hard against the far wall of the quarry. A large lake is present along the entire left side of the hole and fronts the large green.

Cypress Point #16   The best tee-shot in golf! The 16th at Cypress Point is probably the most spectacular hole in the world. The setting is heavenly as you prepare to launch your tee shot across an ocean inlet to a large green set atop a seaside cliff. It offers a delightful potpourri to all your senses, as you smell the salty air, feel the crisp wind, hear the waves crashing and see the contrasting beauty of land, water and sky. It does not get any better.

National Golf Links #17   The 17th plays from a small hill towards Peconic Bay to a green set behind a sand dune. The unkempt beauty of the National Golf Links is set before you in all its' grandeur.

National Golf Links #17

Pebble Beach #18

The 18th at Pebble Beach has all the attributes required for a fine finishing hole and more. It offers a challenging finality to a memorable round, requiring the golfer to muster his courage and skills to finish with a good score. Number 18 is a wonderful risk-reward hole that provides the daring golfer the opportunity to birdie, while punishing the wayward golfer, who is not quite on-top of his game. Most of all, the 18th offers one of the most beautiful settings in the world, hugging the rocky coastline and finishing with the deep blue Pacific Ocean basking at your feet. A dream finish to my Dream 18.

Pebble Beach #18

Tips to Gain Access

Throughout this book I provided a variety of examples of how I gained access to America's most exclusive clubs. Some clubs were very easy to access, while others proved to be very challenging. Many golfers believe they will never have the opportunity to play such courses as Cypress Point, or Pine Valley or especially not Augusta National. They believe it is impossible to meet a member or that the courses are too exclusive to allow non-member guests to play without a member. I have found that only a handful of America's top courses are truly difficult to access, while the rest just require planning and timely execution.

Below I have categorized the array of playing policies I encountered on my journey through the top 100. A significant majority of the top courses offer opportunities to play, without knowing a member, which is good news for most golfers.

The key success factor in my quest was understanding the playing policies and persistently pursuing opportunities to gain entry. I made accessing top courses a priority, allocating time to be available when opportunities were presented.

I also leveraged my personal and professional network to gain entry. You will be surprised how easily it is to network to someone you do not know. At business school we conducted a class exercise to prove a theory that you are rarely more than three relationships away from almost anyone, no matter how famous, in the United States. After doing the exercise, it is amazing to realize the power of your own network. We determined it is possible to meet the President of the United States or Tiger Woods. My own story is proof you do not have to be rich, nor famous to play the best courses in the world. It is all within your grasp.

One disclaimer I need to mention at this time. The playing policies I quote throughout this book were in place during my journey, but they may have changed since the time I played the course. Check with your target club to understand their current policy.

I hope readers will be encouraged and motivated to achieve their own dreams of playing the best courses in America. Do not be intimidated by the "Members Only" sign on the front gate of the best clubs. Be creatively persistent and you will be pleasantly surprised how many great courses you will tick-off your list.

Membership Policies and Access Tips

1. **Must play with a member** --- This is the most challenging playing policy. Most private clubs have between 200 to 450 members who normally live near the course. A few courses have "national" memberships like Augusta National, which means their members are scattered across America or the globe. If you live near a top private course that has a local membership,

meeting a member is not as hard as you may think. You need to first determine the type of member that compose the club. Most courses are filled with successful business people and professionals like lawyers and accountants, who often use their memberships to host clients. You will be surprised at the number of members you or your friends know. Clubs with national memberships are the ultimate challenge, requiring more exposure to a small, influential base of executives. Again though, it is not impossible to meet a member. When I was working at IBM, the President of the company at that time was Lou Gerstner. Lou was a member of Augusta National and would host significant clients to the course on occasion. This is the type of opportunity you must explore for the tough National courses. I have also experienced that members of clubs enjoy hosting you if the occasion for the round is special. They are normally very nice people, who want to be involved with helping others. Events like a college graduation, a father's retirement or a visit from a family member are all good reasons to network to the member.

2. **Member can sponsor play without being present** --- A number of outstanding clubs allow their members to sponsor guests, without being present to play. I leveraged this arrangement to play Cypress Point, Shinnecock Hills and a number of other prestigious clubs. This policy is normally restricted to play during the work week, but a dedicated golfer can normally arrange his/her schedule to accommodate this policy. This policy still requires contact with a member, but a personal relationship with the member is not required, making networking to the member much easier. In fact I played certain courses where I never met the member, like the Honors Course and Seminole. I was able to network through a friend or colleague to obtain permission to play. Again the key is to do a little research and leverage your network.

3. **Host Professional can find a member** --- The next most difficult policy is where the head golf professional at a host club can arrange for you to play with a member. This is normally done for members of other private clubs as a reciprocal arrangement and must be initiated by your head professional. This is actually a nice option, because the host member is normally a nice person, who volunteers to be a host. Many clubs have this policy, including Baltusrol, Interlachen and Scioto. The only drawback is it can take the host professional weeks to find the right pairing, which may impact when you can play.

4. **Club has reciprocal privileges with other private clubs** --- Clubs with this policy are the easiest to access, particularly if you belong to a private club yourself. Many of the great clubs in America have this policy including Prairie Dunes, Oak Tree, Olympia Fields, Stanwich and the Olympic Club. If you are not a member of a private club, have one of your private club friends make the arrangements and tag along for the ride.

5. **Charity events** --- A number of the top clubs in America put their fame to good use by allowing charity events to be played on their course. These events are normally sponsored by members who want to give something back to the community. These charity events offer a wonderful way to access many of the top courses. I leveraged charities to access Castle Pines, Desert Forest, Merion and Peachtree. To find out if the private club you are targeting sponsor's charity events contact the professional at the club. They are normally very happy to provide you the information, so the charity event is a success.

6. **Local Tournaments** --- Some local clubs will sponsor golf tournaments that offer access to non-member golfers. Again, check with the club professional to investigate your options. I played Maidstone and Riviera in local tournaments.

7. **Local National Qualifying** --- For lower handicap golfers there is an opportunity to play the best courses, when they open their gates to host local qualifying for national championships. Any golfer with a handicap below five should investigate this option. Visit the USGA and other golf organization websites to see where the top qualifying rounds are being played. I followed this route to play Camargo and Southern Hills.

8. **New Course Looking for Members** --- On a number of occasions I was able to recognize greatness in the early stages of a course's maturity. During the early years of a club's existence, private clubs are more apt to offer potential members a chance to play the course. I was able to play such courses as Black Diamond Ranch, Sand Hills and the Haig Point Club, by quickly recognizing that these courses were special. When you hear about a new course being built, contact the membership chairman to investigate the possibilities to play the course.

9. **Work the Tournament** --- One unique access offering to mention is that if you work the Masters tournament, as an official, score keeper, concessionaire, range keeper, etc., you are eligible to play the course the following week after the tournament. It is difficult to become one of the select few, but call the club and ask how to get your name on the list. This may also be true for US Open and PGA championship venues as well.

Bibliography

Golf Digest Website
http://www.golfdigest.com/courses/americasgreatest/index.ssf?/courses/americasgreatest/gd200305100greatest.html

500 Greatest Holes in Golf, by George Peper & the Editors of Golf Magazine

The World's Greatest Golf Courses, by Bob Weeks

All photos taken by Dean Sivara

All Scorecards used during rounds at each course

Copy Right – 2009 Version

Made in the USA
San Bernardino, CA
13 January 2013